Praise for Chr
Get Into Class

'If you like classical music and would like to know
more about it, a new guide could help you.
A splendid introduction to enable you
to select your favourite pieces'

Daily Express

'If you need the lowdown on Liszt, the chat on
Tchaikovsky; if you want to be briefed
on Beethoven, primed on Prokofiev,
versed in Vivaldi, this is the
book to read'

What's On

'A nifty little paperback may prove the ideal
gift . . . A non-intimidating introduction
for people who want to know where to
start and what to hear'

Classical Music

'Forget rock, forget rap, pin back your lugholes
and tune into classical music. Grab a copy of
Get Into Classical Music . . . this handy
little book gives you the lowdown and puts a name
to all those familiar tunes you hear
but can't put a name to'

More

'A clever idea well done'

Today

Also by Chris Craker
and published by Bantam Books

Get Into Classical Music
Get Into Opera

Get Into Jazz

Chris Craker

BANTAM BOOKS
TORONTO · NEW YORK · LONDON · SYDNEY · AUCKLAND

GET INTO JAZZ

Based on an original concept by
Chris Craker and Mark Chapple

A BANTAM BOOK : 0 553 40689 2

First Publication in Great Britain

PRINTING HISTORY
Bantam edition published 1994

Set in 11/14½pt Monotype Plantin by Kestrel Data, Exeter

Bantam Books are published by Transworld Publishers Ltd,
61–63 Uxbridge Road, Ealing, London W5 5SA,
in Australia by Transworld Publishers (Australia) Pty Ltd,
15–25 Helles Avenue, Moorebank, NSW 2170,
and in New Zealand by Transworld Publishers (NZ) Ltd,
3 William Pickering Drive, Albany, Auckland.

Reproduced, printed and bound in Great Britain by
Cox & Wyman Ltd, Reading, Berks.

Acknowledgements

My thanks go to Brenda Kimber, Mark Chapple, and my wife Kate whose assistance and support have been invaluable in putting this project together over the past two years.

I would also like to thank Wolfe Muller at Polygram International and Nick and Karen Barnes who provided a safe haven (away from the telephone) in which to write much of this script.

Chris Craker
August 1994

Contents

Preface

For many people jazz is something of a mystery. Most will know the names of Miles Davis, Dizzy Gillespie, Louis Armstrong, Dave Brubeck, Duke Ellington, Count Basie and Oscar Peterson and also the titles of a few famous tunes like 'Take Five', ' 'Round Midnight' and 'O When The Saints', but there is, of course, much more to jazz than these. During the course of the book we shall look at all the main styles of jazz, from ragtime and the blues through to the present day and what is currently happening at jazz clubs and festivals around the world. In conjunction with the CD and cassette *Get Into Jazz*, you'll also be able to get a 'feel' for each of the styles and become acquainted with some of the greatest jazz performers, both singers and instrumentalists.

Although jazz music has been with us for less than a hundred years, its rapid evolution can curiously be likened to the development of a number of other art forms that have spanned many centuries. When one considers how far the medium has travelled stylistically, from the earliest forms to what is being presented today, we can see an obvious parallel with classical music in particular. Throughout the decades, jazz musicians have clearly reflected the mood of their time in much the same way as traditional composers did during the Baroque, Classical, Romantic and Modern eras between 1685 and the present day. Again, like classical music, jazz has until quite recently also been the subject of alienation as a minority interest art form, although a curious form of snobbery has resulted in its being described as 'the devil's music', 'gutter music' or even 'music from the red light district'. Only in the last five years or so has mass interest been reawakened; exciting new artists are emerging, bringing with them a heritage of wonderful music just waiting to be explored.

Those who don't appreciate jazz often consider it cacophonous, meandering, self-indulgent and lacking in form; some even claim it to be performed by promiscuous, wild and drug-addicted weirdos, which in a few cases is quite true, but there we see another intriguing parallel with the world of classical music. One has only to study the lives of characters like Mozart, Beethoven, Liszt and Tchaikovsky to see that very little has changed in terms of the eccentrics that rise to the highest level in their artistic endeavours.

During the course of the book, in addition to exploring the historical development of jazz, we are going to take an in-depth look at the musicians themselves. Unlike most other forms of music where the performers are re-creating performances of other people's music, jazz takes its very soul from the musicians who are playing it: each and every performance of the same tune is completely different by the nature of improvisation – the technique of developing and extending a piece in such a way as to leave one's hallmark on the original tune. There have been, and still are, a whole host of fascinating characters in the world of jazz and it is an impossible task to include everyone's favourite, but I hope that in the course of the book you will be introduced to most of the important artists and also to some of the lesser-known composers, musicians and vocalists who have made a significant contribution to the medium.

One of the most important aspects of this book is the series of 'Recommended Listening' lists that direct you immediately to other tracks and performers that you may well want to hear if your interest has been aroused by what you've heard and read thus far. There are thousands of fine recordings by all the top jazz artists available on CD, record and cassette and the whole jazz legacy is open to us all. The problem that most people face is where exactly to start? Quite often a track on the radio or in a hotel bar catches your attention but you don't know what it is that you're listening to. Even if you do manage to find out the title and you go to your local record store to buy a copy, the chances are that you will be faced either with a blank expression on the other side of the counter (with one or two notable exceptions) or, alternatively, with a bewildering array of different versions from which to choose. That's where this book can come in and offer you some help. I hope it may go some way towards opening up a new world of music for you to enjoy. So, get in the mood, put on the CD or tape and Get Into Jazz.

Chris Craker
August 1994

CHAPTER ONE

Jazz: An Outline History
The First Eighty Years

There is some confusion and dispute about the exact origins of jazz music and there are as many different definitions of the term jazz as there are people that you care to ask. For the purposes of this book, we are going to start right at the beginning, where the first seeds of jazz music started germinating. During the course of about fifteen years around the turn of the century, the appeal of jazz music grew rapidly, spreading from New Orleans to Chicago and New York, eventually reaching the rest of the world once gramophone records and broadcasts were being made available to the public at large.

It is now widely accepted that one of the earliest forms of jazz was based on the music of the ragtime piano players in the southern states of America around 1900. Here follows a tour of the historical development of the jazz movement from that time, when the word was actually spelt 'jass'.

RAGTIME

The style of music known as 'ragtime' emerged in the late nineteenth century in the southern and mid-western states of America. The word ragtime has two suggested sources of derivation: some musicologists see it as linked to the phrase ragged time, i.e. music played freely and with an element of swing, while others think that it has come from the style of black clog dancing known as ragging. This kind of music, whatever the origin of the word, has been aptly described as 'white music played black', i.e. the music is, generally, written down in a formal way but played with a jazzy feel to it. It became especially popular among the labourers engaged in the building of the railroad network in the United States and every bar throughout the southern states would have either a pianist playing rags or a pianola (an automatic piano) playing rolls.

Ragtime was born in Sedalia, Missouri, where the well-known pianist and composer **Scott Joplin** lived, and his name is now synonymous with rag music. Joplin (1868–1917) was born in Texas and settled in Missouri where, along with James Scott (1886–1938) and later Joseph Lamb from New Jersey (1887–1960), he developed this style of music which had its roots in the traditions of late nineteenth-century piano music perhaps best ex-emplified by the works of Louis Moreau Gottschalk (1829–69). Gottschalk was a virtuoso pianist who, at the time, was compared to Franz Liszt – both were prolific composers' and exceptionally talented virtuoso pianists. Joplin and his colleagues were familiar with the works of Gottschalk and they also derived inspiration from the marches, polonaises and works based on folk themes by the great romantic classical composers Frederic Chopin and Franz Liszt.

Rag music is invariably in duple time (i.e. music written in 2/4 or 4/4 time) and, harmonically, the chords used are generally restricted to simple harmonies based upon the first, fourth and fifth degrees of the scale (the tonic, sub-dominant and dominant). Syncopation (*see* p.29) plays a big part in this music; the fast-moving tune in the right hand of the piano is set against a strong rhythmic figuration in the left hand (this technique is sometimes referred to as 'stride piano'). The sustaining pedal on the piano was used very little so the music always sounded punchy and rhythmic. Indeed, sometimes the foot would be called upon to stamp in time with the music, as in Joplin's 'Stoptime Rag', written in 1910. The manner of performance of rags has been the subject of some contention among musicians and musicologists. Scott Joplin frequently printed at the top of the manuscript paper 'Notice! Don't play this piece fast. It is never right to play "Ragtime" fast. Author.' As this has been written by the acknowledged 'King' of Ragtime composers, one must assume that it holds some authority. However, I am prepared to confront the critics and say that many rags sound fantastically exciting when played at breakneck speed and exceedingly dull when played 'straight' and slow – it's all a matter of personal taste. Joshua Rifkin, an American historian and musicologist, subscribes to the authentic manner of performance and there are dozens of

3

recordings to sample if this style appeals to you.

The first composition published using the title of 'Rag' was ironically not by Scott Joplin. 'The Mississippi Rag' was written by William H. Krell, a Chicago bandleader who toured around the Mississippi region. There is an enormous amount of ragtime music available in print, but it is the works of Scott Joplin that have really captured the public's attention. He wrote more than six hundred rags, several of which have become 'standards' made particularly popular by their inclusion in the 1973 film *The Sting*: the most famous pieces are 'The Entertainer' and the 'Maple Leaf Rag'.

Rag music was the first black music to have a truly worldwide influence – even classical composers such as Claude Debussy incorporated ragtime style in 'The Golliwog's Cakewalk' from his *Children's Corner Suite*. Ragtime went on to develop stylistically with the aid of musicians like **Jelly Roll Morton** (1890–1941), who felt restricted and confined by the rigid structure of the ragtime piano pieces. Apparently Morton's performances of Joplin's works were very free and more jazzy in style than is considered acceptable these days. Morton can be considered one of the fathers of the New Orleans school of jazz that developed in the early part of the twentieth century.

NEW ORLEANS JAZZ, DIXIELAND AND THE BLUES

New Orleans at the turn of the century must have been a fascinating place to be. The extraordinarily diverse mixture of cultures and races inevitably gave rise to a wealth of cross-cultural fertilization, particularly in music. Prior to the Louisiana Purchase, the city had been under French and Spanish rule and so, in addition to the French and Spanish, English people, Italians, Germans and Slavs were all living together alongside the numerous Africans whose ancestors had been brought over as slaves. Everyone wanted to hold fast to their own musical roots and this, coupled with the rise of Christianity (and the consequent singing of hymns and spirituals), gave ample scope for each and every nation, race and religion to be musically represented somewhere along the line. The staggering statistic that there were more than thirty orchestras in Delta City by 1910, from a population of just over 200,000 people, is hard to believe, but undeniably demonstrates a high degree of commitment to music as an essential part of life.

Out of the various musical styles, an identifiable 'New Orleans sound' developed towards the end of the first decade of this century. Typically based on a march-like tempo and rhythm, the music always sounded intense and expressive. It was invariably joyous in spirit and the rhythm section, consisting of a string or brass bass, drums, banjo or guitar and sometimes a piano, provided the backbone of the music: this would then be embellished by three front-line instrumentalists, normally clarinet, trumpet (or cornet) and trombone, each improvising lines that intertwined with each other to form a colourful collage of sound.

Although the stereotype picture of a New Orleans 'Dixieland' jazz band is one of a group of coloured players, jazz was by no means the sole property of the Afro-Americans, indeed there are records of all-white jazz bands dating back to the last decade of the nineteenth century. George Vitelle Laine (commonly known as **'Papa' Laine**) was hailed as the first white jazz musician and he formed a number of very fine bands who performed all over the United States. There were, however, two distinct styles of playing: white jazz was generally technically more ordered and the sound of the music as a whole was considered by many to be less expressive, while the black jazz used 'blue' (more exotic) harmonies and was generally more soulful in character. The earliest exponents of Dixieland jazz who have been extensively recorded were the appropriately titled **Original Dixieland Jazz Band** (or the ODJB, as it became known) which was a group formed by Nick La Rocca.

When the very best bands from the southern states of America started to tour, their recordings became available internationally and broadcasts of their work were enjoyed by relatively large audiences. The ODJB made its debut at the Reisenweber's Cabaret in New York in 1917, after which their recordings sold millions of copies. It's interesting to note that in this very year, while the ODJB were enjoying an unprecedented degree of success, Scott Joplin died almost unnoticed, such was the change in the public's taste and interest.

By 1921 jazz enjoyed mass popularity and a huge influx of recordings was flooding the market; young artists like the inimitable trumpeter **Louis Armstrong** hit the scene, alongside musicians like pianist **Earl 'Fatha' Hines**, soprano saxophonist and clarinettist **Sidney Bechet** and the young cornet player **Bix Beiderbecke** who were all making their mark on the jazz scene. The extraordinarily named Ferdinand Joseph Le Menthe **'Jelly Roll'**

6

Morton was still very much around and is undoubtedly regarded as one of the finest exponents of jazz piano from these early days. He was reputed to be an extremely colourful character – as well as being a fine pianist, he was a composer, a pool shark, a comedian and a pimp! He also claimed to be the 'inventor of jazz', an extravagant claim which nevertheless has some truth in it, for many of his works are now standards and the recordings that were made in the early twenties do bear the hallmarks of a truly innovative, creative and influential musician.

BLUES AND BOOGIE WOOGIE

Jazz in New Orleans had the most important influence on the development of jazz all around the United States, Chicago in particular. During the 1920s, bands in Chicago and New York started to develop identities of their own, taking elements of a number of styles to create their own hybrids: the two most significant of these other styles that were performed and developed throughout the first twenty years of the century were the Blues and Boogie Woogie. The word 'blues' can be traced back as far as 1853, when a Boston newspaper advocated that one should indulge in light reading to lift the spirits of those suffering from the 'blues' or 'ennui' – the blues meaning a state of depression or despondency. However, the first use of this term to describe music is not found until 1910, after which time it became increasingly more common.

Stylistically, blues music adheres to a number of set patterns: the basic twelve-bar chord structure has been consistent right from the earliest days to the most developed form of the blues which is performed today. The chord structures are simple and the melodies that feature above them take their character from the music of the black musicians brought from Africa to the New World. Their music was largely based on a pentatonic scale (i.e. a scale employing just five notes) but when opened to the influences of the European music in America a new tonal sense developed that included the addition of the third and seventh degrees of the scale to their pentatonic version. A straight major scale sounded bland and characterless to their ears and so these third and seventh degrees of the scale were flattened (i.e. made one semitone lower) which provide us with the 'blue' notes in the blues scale on which all such music is now based. This soulful, melancholic music utilizes all the normal compositional devices that are employed in all other kinds of music (including classical) to establish and convey the desired mood – descending melodic lines and slow-moving harmonies are the most important traits, while the lyrics sung to blues songs almost always focus on suffering, loss and heartbreak, although there are some examples of humorous and happy blues pieces, too.

The earliest exponents of blues music included the singers **Mamie Smith** (whose first recording of 'Crazy Blues' in 1920 went on to be an all-time best-seller), **Ma Rainey** and the 'Queen of the Blues', **Bessie Smith**, who was born in 1895. More recent singers who have achieved worldwide fame include **Ella Fitzgerald** and **Sarah Vaughan**, while some of the most illustrious in- strumentalists involved in the blues are **B. B. King**, **Fats Waller** and the legendary **John Lee Hooker**, who sang 'I've got the blues so bad, it's hard to keep me from cryin' ' – a classic line that encapsulates, rather poetically, the true sentiment behind the blues.

Originally called 'the fast Western blues', boogie woogie is the style of jazz that developed during the late 1920s in the South Side of Chicago. It is characterized by the driving, eight-to-the-bar, left-hand piano riffs with simple, repetitive melodies over the top. It is now thought of mainly as a piano style but some of the earliest forms did develop from banjo and guitar figures. **Clarence 'Pinetop' Smith** is credited with having given this style of music its name. Smith was born in Alabama but lived in Chicago and wrote the celebrated piece 'Pinetop's Boogie Woogie'.

SWING AND BIG BAND

Towards the end of the 1920s a number of factors had a significant effect on the overall feel and style of jazz music – some of these rose out of the musical instincts of the players involved, while others were a result of the social and political climate at the time. The first major change that took place was due to the almost unanimous desire to move away from two-beat jazz; musicians felt the need to break the established traditions of 2/4 and 4/4 beat music (two beats or four beats to the bar) in favour of something new and rhythmically different. Secondly, the economic conditions of the time, with the Wall Street Crash having sent the US economy into a state of complete turmoil, led to huge numbers of musicians and people in the entertainment industry being put out of work, and those that were still performing therefore had to find something new and exciting with which to stimulate their audiences. Moreover whatever audience there was for such entertainment was very hard pushed to find the money to pay for it. This was a critical time and an undoubted turning point in the history of the entertainment industry. Popular songs and sentimental ballads became the favourites and the musicians that survived this period were generally in bands that were prepared to provide music for a wider, more middle-of-the-road audience who also wanted to dance.

So it was that Swing Bands and numerous dance bands were formed, while the smaller, more intense-sounding jazz combos (five- and six-piece bands) were still active, but became less fashionable. Because the music was now to be played by much larger forces, a new format and structure to the music was required. The musicians required more formal, written-out parts from which to play – a ten- or fifteen-piece band all doing their own thing could have interesting consequences! This, in turn, gave rise to the need for a new breed of musician – the arranger. The arranger was required to write and arrange the parts for the band. His job not only involved the mechanical task of writing out the notes to be played but also added a significant creative input, as he had free rein to alter the structure of the piece (even change the tune slightly, if he so wished) and to decide on the combinations of instruments that should be playing at any one time. He was also the one who decided when players would be given the opportunity to take a solo and this inevitably gave less room for spontaneous creative contributions from the individual members of the group. In order to balance this rather stifling trend for the really creative players, it was common for bands to consist of two types of musician: the well-schooled type and one or two 'hot' soloists (usually sax and trumpet players) who would take a chorus of the piece to improvise on, so that some real jazz playing could be incorporated in what many of the jazz purists might have seen as a stylistic turn for the worse.

Although, for many, this period was seen as a time of more formalization within the jazz genre, a number of highly talented and innovative giants from the world of jazz emerged, including **Duke Ellington**, **Count Basie**, **Benny Goodman**, **Don Redman**, **Gene Krupa** and **Glenn Miller**. All these artists, and many others like them, had a unique gift for making music 'swing'. The word swing is another term used in jazz that causes some confusion – it really has two meanings and it's important to clarify these at this point. In the first instance, swing is the name given to a generic style of music that became popular in the 1930s. However, the term swing can also be used as an adjective to describe the feel or 'groove' of a piece, which comes from the inherent natural rhythm that gives the music its overall character. Jazz purists and commentators are very particular about whether musicians or particular pieces of music 'swing' and it's such an important aspect of jazz music that it seems appropriate to include here the phrase from Duke Ellington's celebrated masterpiece, 'It don't mean a thing, if it ain't got that swing . . .'

Bennie Moten was one of the pioneers of the big band movement. He was active in the Kansas City area and developed a style of playing that incorporated large, showy arrangements of popular tunes, giving the whole band an opportunity to carry the lead line at the same time, in syncopated, harmonized, highly rhythmic patterns or riffs, as they became known. This style of playing and arranging became identifiable as Kansas City Swing and was later taken a stage or two further by people like Count Basie, while **Duke Ellington**, on the other hand, developed and expanded his works into quite complex compositions, giving his highly talented soloists ample opportunity to show off their prowess on their individual instruments through improvised soloing. Ellington was surrounded by an abundance of pure genius in his band, which included such illustrious musicians as the sax players Ben Webster, Johnny Hodges, Harry Carney and Don Redman, and the trumpeters Dizzy Gillespie, Clark Terry and Cootie Williams; these players and others earned the Ellington band the reputation of comprising the 'hottest' soloists around.

One cannot talk about swing music without mention of the 'King of Swing', the clarinettist **Benny Goodman**. Goodman's band was polished, professional and exciting under the leadership of the great man himself with his unique gift for stylish and fluent improvisations. He was very well schooled in music, having studied earnestly in a rather classical tradition and his band was made up of similarly well-versed players who produced a new, rather refined style of jazz. If any criticism may be levelled, it is that the improvisations of his band members err on the more formal and sterile side (being closely based around scales and arpeggios); however, because of the players' sheer technical brilliance, the tempos of Goodman's tunes gradually became faster and faster and a new sense of excitement and rhythmic vitality was injected into the medium of swing that did much to earn Benny Goodman his totally justifiable title, 'The King of Swing'.

Count Basie was another leading figure, whose band of the Thirties played an eclectic mixture of all the current styles. He was renowned for surrounding himself with a superb team of professionals, including the legendary Lester Young on tenor saxophone. Basie's bands (he led many with varying line-ups and changes of personnel) were punchy and exciting. There are plenty of recordings to enjoy and the sheer impact of the brass and saxophones in his stunning arrangements are beautifully complemented by the refined, exquisite, tinkling riffs of Basie's piano.

Another celebrated band leader that created a unique sound within his musical arrangements was **Glenn Miller**, who died tragically on the night of 15 December 1944. What made Miller's band sound unique was the subtle doubling of the lead line between the saxophone section and a lone clarinet. Miller managed to break into the mainstream commercial market quite quickly with such all-time favourites as 'Moonlight Seranade', 'Little Brown Jug' and 'In The Mood'. His loss in the immediate postwar years was deeply felt by both the music profession and the general public. Although he was not considered to be on a musical par with characters like Ellington and Basie, Glenn Miller brought to big band music enormous energy and romance that was appreciated by the very widest audience; his music remains popular to this day.

During this time recording techniques were progressing rapidly and the musicians themselves began to be dissatisfied with the more commercial, middle-of-the-road line that jazz music was beginning to take. Many musicians and their audiences turned to nostalgic revivals of ragtime, Dixieland and 'hot' jazz. Yet it was obvious to many that another jazz revolution was about to take place. Some new instruments were becoming fashionable, such as the electric guitar and the vibraphone, while the technical proficiency, the vision and ambition of the musicians were themselves enough to spawn the new style known as bebop.

BEBOP

Bebop is the word used to describe the style of jazz that emerged in the 1940s and the immediate postwar period. The origin of the word is, again, the subject of much debate among jazz aficionados, but it is commonly accepted that the word derives from the sound made by jazz musicians vocalizing and singing instrumental lines with nonsense syllables – a technique otherwise known as 'scat' singing, originally pioneered by Louis Armstrong. Bebop developed because a number of jazz musicians felt that swing, and big band music in general, were too restricting and limiting in their power of expression. Many felt that the whole jazz movement was in a rut and needed an injection of new life that would release their individual creative talents, as had the introduction of narcotics to their own lifestyles! Some, too, wanted to rebel against the rather tired, old-fashioned, image of the early New Orleans jazz musicians and were the 'punks' of their day, heralding a time of change.

All the characteristics of early bebop (or bop, as it is sometimes referred to) were developed further: chord progressions and harmonies became more adventurous, rhythms and tempos were employed that broke new ground in their sheer speed and inventiveness, melodies ignored the established traditions and, most importantly, greater scope was given to the soloist to be free in improvisation. The underlying desire of many of the musicians themselves was to form a new élite style of jazz that would be seen to be a real art form and a more serious means of creative expression. There was a sense of frustration with the whole 'show band' scene – but remember, swing and dance band music were still popular and very much alive. The swing scene didn't stop overnight for one very good reason: the public still enjoyed it and it was a commercial money spinner for the record companies, broadcasting authorities and, to a lesser extent, the bands themselves.

Just as New Orleans had been the centre of jazz during the Twenties, Harlem became a haven for the new set of jazz revolutionaries. Minton's Playhouse (a converted china warehouse in West 118th Street in Harlem) and Monroe's Uptown House were among the most famous jazz 'hangouts' and it was at these venues that many of the now famed bebop jazz exponents made their mark. Bebop, invariably played by small combo bands of from three to six players, was dramatically different from the established forms of jazz being played at the time. The musical characteristics that identify bebop music are many: the bass player provides the essential backbone of the music by way of a constant beat, while the drummer is mainly confined to driving the music along with an incessant ride cymbal rhythm, utilizing the rest of the kit for shock accents or fills as required, as best exemplified by drummers in the mould of Kenny Clarke and Max

Roach. All the other instruments then play their varying roles as soloists, employing quite stylized melodic patterns and riffs, predominantly using the interval of the flattened fifth. Just as the blues scale used the flattened third and seventh degrees of the scale to set its musical feel and character, so the interval between the first and the flattened fifth degrees was employed to set the tone of much bebop music. This whole business of relationships between notes in the scale is what gives every style of music its individual character, in just the same way that spoken languages all rely on the sounds of the alphabet and the relationship between consonants and syllables to establish the identifiable words and sounds that make up a language.

Among the best-known exponents in the early days of bebop were **Charlie Parker** (saxophone), **Thelonious Monk** (piano), **Dizzy Gillespie** (trumpet), **Kenny Clarke** (drums) and **Charlie Christian** (guitar) – profiles of the first four of these artists, and many of the other 'greats' from this period of jazz, follow in Chapter Four. Their influence on the whole spectrum of bebop is immeasurable; in particular, people like John Coltrane, Sonny Rollins and later, Sonny Stitt, Lee Konitz, Phil Woods, Art Pepper and many others who experienced this latest development of the greatest traditions of jazz playing were enabled to carry on where their forerunners left off.

During the mid-Forties, the swing bands that were still active and enjoying success alongside the bebop revolutionaries started to take the whole band style a step further by introducing elements of bebop into the big band sound. Among the bands that followed this line were **Woody**

Herman's Band and those of **Stan Kenton, Boyd Raeburn** and **Earl Spencer**; all of them paved the way for talented saxophonists like Stan Getz, Zoot Sims and Al Cohn.

'Modern Jazz' was now established and interesting developments took place during this period and towards the end of the Forties. It was just into the early part of the 1950s that it became apparent that a new breed of jazz player was emerging and clamouring to be heard.

AFRO-CUBOP AND LATIN JAZZ

The African settlers in the Caribbean held fast to their musical roots and their influence has been widely felt on the whole jazz movement. After the First World War many Cuban immigrants made their way to the United States, among them the great jazz musicians **Rod Rodriguez, Juan Tizol** and **Alberto Socarras**. Their infectious enthusiasm for the music they held so close to their hearts was immediately attractive to many in the bebop movement. They found the idea of incorporating Cuban polyrhythms into their music, as well as the traditional South American percussion instruments, an extremely exciting prospect. Latin Jazz was born and a number of different strands developed, invariably based upon regional variations of dance styles, like the bossa nova, samba and tango.

Many of the most important musicians who made their mark in this field were either percussion players or trumpeters. **Mario Bauza** left Havana to settle in New York and worked both as a player and as an arranger with, amongst others, Dizzy Gillespie and another great South

American musician, **Machito**. Born in 1912, Machito (whose real name was Raul Grillo) was a percussionist and bandleader who moved to New York in 1927, where he eventually founded his own orchestra. This became known as one of the finest Afro-Cuban outfits in town and Machito invited a whole host of guest stars to appear with the band, including Charlie Parker, Dexter Gordon, Dizzy Gillespie and Julian 'Cannonball' Adderley.

Chico O'Farrill is another Cuban trumpeter who made a significant impact on the big band scene, being one of the favourite arrangers for Benny Goodman, Stan Kenton, Count Basie, Clark Terry and Dizzy Gillespie, who were all very much taken by his exotic, orchestral style of writing. Other great talents of this time include **Chano Pozo**, **Mongo Santamaria**, **Tito Puente**, **Perez Prado**, **Charlie** and **Eddie Palmieri** and **Paquito D'Rivera**; they were a source of inspiration for the better-known mainstream jazz performers like Charlie Parker, Dizzy Gillespie, Thelonious Monk, Chick Corea and Herbie Hancock.

More recently, the incredible Cuban trumpeter **Arturo Sandoval**, who was a co-founder of the band Irakere, emerged as one of the world's leading jazz attractions – I use the word 'attraction' deliberately, as Sandoval is more than a fine musician. He is a virtuoso player who seems to be able to play at least two octaves higher on the trumpet than anyone else I've ever heard and manages to entertain an audience in a very individual way, keeping them on the edge of their seats from start to finish. He took part in the film *A Night in Havana* with Dizzy Gillespie, and this, coupled with his numerous appearances at festivals and jazz clubs all around the world, has ensured that Cubop is now very firmly part of mainstream jazz music.

COOL JAZZ

The proliferation of so many different jazz schools, from old style swing bands like Glenn Miller's to the distinctive sounds of the bands of Kenton, Basie and Ellington, gave further impulse to musicians who wanted to move away from the commercial rat race and set their own styles. As jazz moved into the 1950s, there was no one style or school of jazz that could be labelled 'mainstream'. All those musicians who were not part of one of the 'name' bands were desperately seeking new idioms and devices to forge a way ahead in the jazz movement.

Cool Jazz was one of the first new styles to make its mark at this time – a style of playing founded by people like **Stan Getz**, **Lennie Tristano**, **Tadd Dameron**, **Gerry Mulligan**, **Johnny Carisi**, **John Lewis** and **Miles Davis**. Getz, Tristano and Davis were among the most influential, each in a different way: Getz had been in the business since the age of fifteen and had been through the star-studded days with the Kenton Band, having also played with Jimmy Dorsey and Benny Goodman, but it was following his period in the Woody Herman band that his unique style of delivery was perceived to be something quite unusual and influential. His sound was frequently described as 'cool', clean and haunting, and was very different from the sounds produced by the legendary Charlie Parker and Coleman Hawkins – full-toned, bebop boys who could play with an edge that would cut relentlessly through any band.

Tristano was one of the jazz radicals – he was highly intelligent, outspoken and forthright in his views on what was happening in the jazz scene at the time. His music was among the most revolutionary of the styles that were emerging around 1950, with harmonic progressions and a degree of complexity within the contrapuntal lines that had not been presented before. **Miles Davis** formed his own orchestra and recorded an album on 21 January 1949, which claimed it to be the Birth of the Cool; while this suggests it may have been the real landmark recording of the time, it was, in fact, quite an experimental project that featured the arrangements of Gil Evans and Gerry Mulligan. The orchestrations were very unusual in their inclusion of the french horn and the tuba. It was because of works like this that an even newer form of jazz emerged that came to be known as Third Stream. It really involved an infusion of musicians from the classical world, but its success was limited for a number of reasons: on the one hand the idea of jazz being written down note for note and performed by musicians who were not brought up with jazz in their blood seemed, for many, incongruous. However, musicians like the horn player **Gunther Schuller** (from the Metropolitan Opera in New York) presented a number of interesting concerts and recording projects which achieved a certain degree of popularity and influence. Schuller created new sounds and brought together musicians from diverse backgrounds, firing the imaginations of many in the jazz world around him.

The whole business of labelling varying styles East and West Coast was really dreamt up by the marketing departments of the record companies – and it was, indeed, a very successful device that produced massive sales of recordings. However, in reality, musicians like Getz and Mulligan were really just getting on with their own thing and had no interest in any kind of labels or schools of jazz. West Coast jazz was the term most commonly linked with the Miles Davis/Capitol Records sessions and all the associated bands and smaller combinations that followed his lead. East Coast, and those playing bop in New York, appeared to move on from bebop to 'hard bop', when their music became even more committed and direct in its expression. **John Coltrane** was one of the leaders of the hard bop scene – his music sounded so extreme that it seemed quite alien to many. Tempos became faster, the music louder and ballads more and more intense, and it was at this time in the faster tracks that the term 'funky' came into common use. Funky music bore some close relationships to the blues and gospel music and the singer **Ray Charles** was one of the first to bring these elements together to the most marvellous effect. Many fine musicians emerged at this time alongside Coltrane; they include **Horace Silver**, **Art Blakey**, **Sonny Rollins**, **Chet Baker** and a host of others, some of whose lives make for interesting reading in Chapter Four.

Going one stage further, two groups emerged that met with universal appeal because of their inimitable blend of styles, the **Modern Jazz Quartet** and the **Dave Brubeck Quartet**. The Modern Jazz Quartet (MJQ) was formed in 1951 and toured the concert circuit presenting music that combined the elements of the most refined schools of bebop, West Coast and Third Stream. The MJQ was made up of four highly intelligent and talented musicians: John Lewis (piano), Milt Jackson (vibraphone), Percy Heath (bass) and Kenny Clarke (drums). Dave Brubeck's quartet featured the celebrated Paul Desmond on alto saxophone and Joe Morello on drums and toured extensively (initially throughout the college circuit in the USA) to unanimous approval. Brubeck's music crossed over into classical realms, using classical themes as in 'Blue Rondo A La Turk'. The tune that everyone will be familiar with is 'Take Five', which was set in the unusual time of five beats to the bar but nevertheless captured the imagination of musicians and the public alike.

JAZZ SAMBA

Just as the Cubop movement made an enormous impact on mainstream jazz, so did the emergence of music springing directly from Brazil. In the clubs of Rio de Janeiro during the late Forties, jazz samba was the music of the moment – great for dancing and immediately attractive as a 'party' kind of music. It rapidly gained many followers when the trend spread to the United States. Musicians like the multi-instrumentalist **Pixinghas** had already prepared the ground by presenting 'chorro' music (a traditional kind of Brazilian blues) and **Johnny Alf, Antonio Carlos 'Tom' Jobim** and **Joao Gilberto** took things a stage further, establishing the bossa nova and samba as the main Latin styles that lent themselves well to a jazz idiom. These both met with wide success and have grown even more in popularity over the last thirty years.

Gilberto and his wife **Astrud**, had huge hits with 'The Girl From Ipanema' and 'Desafinado' in the Sixties, and demonstrated to the jazz aficionados that artists like the great tenor saxophonist Stan Getz could join in and make a serious statement through this medium. Similar in approach to the cool music of the more serious side of jazz, in their economy of expression and the feelings they evoke, jazz samba and bossa nova have many fans both in the jazz world and now in the middle-of-the-road mass market.

FREE JAZZ

The term Free Jazz was employed because the music of the early Sixties that subscribed to this school, was exactly that – totally free from any form of constraint, either rhythmically, harmonically or instrumentally. A similar turn of events was happening in the classical music field at this time, too, and even though jazz musicians like **Ornette Coleman** and **Charlie Mingus** received very mixed reactions, their move towards avant-garde jazz was relatively mild in comparison with the 'reactionary' classical composers of the day. Championed on the one hand by progressive musicians and commentators, the work of Coleman and his compatriots was abhorrent to many who preferred to stick to the more traditional jazz music and values represented by people like the MJQ and the pianist **Oscar Peterson**.

Historically there is an interesting parallel to be drawn between this new 'free jazz' movement and the breakaway from traditional ragtime to the New Orleans Dixieland style, where the musicians were given space to improvise and play lines crossing each other with complex con-trapuntal results. It was, however, the distinct move away from a sense of key structure and tonal harmony that most people found difficult to accept – a move which had its counterpart in literary and art worlds with the forfeiture of grammatical sensibility in literature, and traditional formal design and drawing in contemporary works of art.

Jazz musicians looked to other cultures to find inspiration and **John Coltrane** was among the most successful in this. He turned to devices used in Indian music: repetition of rhythmic patterns devoid of any traditional harmonic roots. This led to such classic tracks as 'Giant Steps' in 1959 and 'A Love Supreme' some years later. **Stan Getz** was drawn towards South American and Latin influences and in 1963 produced a wonderful album in *Jazz Samba*. The track 'Desafinado' is now one of the all-time classic standards in the jazz genre and put bossa nova firmly on the map, while drawing a new audience to accessible, foot-tapping jazz that was very easy on the ear.

Some musicians still wanted to hold fast to what had gone before and build upon tried and tested genres of music. The prime example is virtuoso trumpeter **Maynard Ferguson** who had a prestigious start to his musical career playing in the Stan Kenton Band in the late Forties and early Fifties. Ferguson's own big band toured extensively and created its own unique identity (hallmarked by the extraordinary stratospheric trumpet playing of its leader) to great popular and critical acclaim. However, it was the move towards electronics, synthesizers and contemporary production techniques that alienated many traditional jazz fans and, for many jazz buffs, 'real jazz' stopped in about 1969.

Throughout the Sixties and into the Seventies musicians like the trumpeter Freddie Hubbard, pianist/band leader Stan Tracey, composer Mike Westbrook and a whole host of others broke fascinating new ground by bringing together the sources of their inspiration into a new, contemporary context. Those pillars of the jazz fraternity **Miles Davis** and **Dizzy Gillespie** and their like continued on their journeys, exploring the fascinating world of jazz and its many derivatives with great commercial success. Miles Davis in particular moved into completely new areas of music and proved a source of much inspiration for musicians from all backgrounds. He was drawn into music for films and became a real cult figure in the music industry.

JAZZ ROCK

In the early Seventies, musicians who had been influenced by such luminaries as Miles Davis, Charlie Parker, Dizzy Gillespie and John Coltrane, went on to break new ground with a new form of jazz known as jazz-rock fusion or, when using more electric and synthesized sounds, 'electro-jazz-rock fusion'. Some of Miles Davis's sidemen, **Josef (Joe) Zawinul** and **Wayne Shorter,** joined forces to form a band called Weather Report – one of the most important groups to emerge at this time. Guitarist **John McLaughlin** formed the Mahavishnu Orchestra, while **Chick Corea, Herbie Hancock, Gary Burton, Soft Machine** and the **Charles Lloyd Quartet** forged their own ways ahead in various directions. Elements of pure rock music crept in, including the use of more and more electric instruments and contemporary production techniques. However, towering over all these highly talented 'youngsters' was the genius of **Miles Davis,** who really captured the essence of jazz and rock in his album *Bitches Brew* which was released as early as 1970. Multi-track recording techniques and the use of synthesizers and time delay techniques were now becoming a matter of course and some instrumentalists, like **Sonny Stitt** and **Lee Konitz**, even started to process the sounds of their own acoustic instruments by the use of ring modulators, pitch shifters, octave dividers and phase shifters, creating the most extraordinary effects that would never have been dreamt of just a few years earlier.

Jazz Rock music has many guises; later in the book we'll look more closely at some of the styles adopted, as they have become more formalized in the last ten years or so – *see* Chapter Three. We'll also consider what effects the developments of the first eighty years of jazz have had on music today.

CHAPTER TWO

'Your Starter Selection'
The Music on the CD and cassette
Get Into Jazz

The CD and cassette that are available in conjunction with this book contain eighteen tracks by many of the world's finest jazz artists. By listening to the recordings as you read through the book you will become acquainted with both the sounds of some of these performers and, equally importantly, a selection of the wide variety of styles of jazz that there are to be explored.

The tracks chosen demonstrate most of the main styles of jazz (it's impossible to include a sample of everything), starting from a first taste of ragtime piano music and ending with some recent music written, recorded and performed by Joe Henderson in 1992; we take in some trad, swing, bebop, cool, modern, Latin and electro-jazz fusion along the way. Some tracks are what are called 'standards', i.e. tunes that people all around the world are familiar with. These tunes have since been performed by countless other performers in a variety of genres (not necessarily jazz) and they are pieces that many will have heard without knowing the title. It's every composer's dream to write a standard (the royalty payments can become quite significant!) and tunes like 'Summertime', 'Stardust', 'Body and Soul', 'It Don't Mean a Thing If It Ain't Got That Swing', 'Tangerine' and 'My Funny Valentine' are good examples. Standards are an essential part of every jazz musician's repertoire – all the great jazz performers commit such tunes to memory and are familiar with their chord structures so that they are able to improvise freely, confident of the direction that the tune is taking. This allows the musician the utmost creative freedom, which is, after all, the very essence of jazz.

At the end of the description and background information on each track featured on the CD and cassette, I've given a few recommendations as to other recordings that you may enjoy if the piece in question has attracted your attention. It would add to your enjoyment and understanding to listen to some of these as you make your way through the book, although it's not imperative. Catalogue numbers of the recordings are included so that tracking them down will be that much easier. So, here follows a brief introduction to the essential jazz styles and to the tracks on the accompanying CD and cassette; subsequent chapters will serve to widen your experience.

RAGTIME

'*Climax Rag*' (written by James Scott)
performed by Ralph Sutton, piano

Hailing from the very beginning of the twentieth century, 'Climax Rag' contains all the classic hallmarks of ragtime piano music and is brilliantly played here by the celebrated pianist Ralph Sutton who went into the studio in 1949 to record a number of pieces closely associated with the great Jelly Roll Morton. Rag music was originally played only on the piano as here, but later, small bands of four or five instrumentalists played more colourful arrangements of this type of music. Many will be familiar with rag music as made famous in the film *The Sting*, in which some of the works of Scott Joplin were featured – probably the two most famous pieces are 'The Entertainer' and 'The Maple Leaf Rag'.

'Climax Rag' contains an excellent example of 'stride piano' playing, typical in rag music, where the left hand is required to play a bass note with the little finger (on the first and third beats of the bar) and quickly jump up to the middle of the piano to play a chord on the off beats. this gives a great solid rhythm to the piece over which the right hand plays a virtuoso, 'syncopated' tune. 'Syncopation' is the term used to describe a simple musical line or tune that is disrupted by the beat being delayed or accented – it is a musical device that is extremely common in all jazz music and is essential to the way that the music swings. On this evocative recording you can also hear Ralph Sutton singing along to the music in a kind of 'scat' style. This is a technique of singing that has no words, but simply employs varied vocal sounds like 'scat-'n-'dit-'n-'dat' or 'hi-de-hi-de-ho'. Two of the most famous scat singers were Louis Armstrong and Cab Calloway, while more recent exponents include the singer Cleo Laine and the guitarist George Benson who vocally 'mirrors' his improvised guitar solos, creating a fascinating effect.

'Climax Rag' on this recording perfectly captures the atmosphere and spirit of rag music and if you're attracted to this style it would be well worth investigating the works of Scott Joplin, Joseph Lamb, James Scott and Jelly Roll Morton, whose music was also based upon rags and stomp music and is highly recommended. There is a large and interesting catalogue of both original and new recordings, but here are three favourites of mine that are also examples of the very best rag music.

RECOMMENDED LISTENING

Digital Ragtime
EMI: TCEMD 5534 (CD)

Jelly Morton's Jams
Verve: 517 777-2 (CD)

Le Ragtime de Scott Joplin
Arion: ARN 64022 (CD)

DIXIELAND

'Ballin' The Jack'
(written by J. Burriss/ C. Smith)
performed by The Ken Colyer Band

Moving on to Dixieland jazz and the music of New Orleans and Chicago in the late Twenties, Ken Colyer's Band playing 'Ballin' The Jack' is a fine example of music in this style. A typical Dixieland band line-up includes trumpet, clarinet, trombone, piano, bass (either string or brass), drums and banjo. The tunes are often stomps, rags or blues-based and you can hear this type of jazz in many jazz pubs and clubs all over the world. There are literally hundreds of records to explore by all the great trad and dixieland jazz bands; many early original recordings are available as well as the more up-to-date albums by well-known artists like Kenny Ball, Acker Bilk, Chris Barber and Humphrey Lyttelton.

Recorded in August, 1960, 'Ballin' The Jack' is a Dixieland stomp tune that features the wonderful sounds of Sammy Remington on clarinet and Ken Colyer on trumpet. It's interesting to see how this style of music developed from the early ragtime piano pieces some ten or twenty years previously, where the pianist was left alone to provide both the tune and the accompaniment – the 'stride piano' technique has already been described and now, from within the rhythm section of the Dixieland jazz band, the task of providing this effect is split between the drums, bass, banjo and piano. The bass player normally provides a stomping four beats to the bar together with the banjo, while the drummer is free to play a simple stomp rhythm or to add interesting fills and percussion sounds. The pianist can also just go along with the rhythm section by way of accompaniment during the verses, and then take a solo passage as Ray Foxley does in this arrangement of 'Ballin' The Jack'.

The Ken Colyer Band is famous for producing a traditional 'Dixieland' sound, even though they are British, and each of the players has a very authentic-sounding timbre to their instruments: the clarinettist plays with a nice edge that cuts through the 'thick' texture of the band and the trumpet has a raspy vibrato that is so typical of this style of music, though it would be unacceptable in any other. The trombonist provides the wonderful sliding motifs that lead us from the verses into the chorus and bridge passages of the tune, while the banjo, bass and drums stomp their way through the track in true Dixieland spirit.

RECOMMENDED LISTENING

Compact Jazz: The Best of Dixieland
Verve: 831 375-2 (CD)

Dixieland Collection
Deja Vu: DVCD 2119 (CD)

The Guv'nor 1959–1961
Polydor: 830 782-2 (CD)

'Someday You'll Be Sorry'
(written by Louis Armstrong)
performed by The Louis Armstrong Band

'Some Day You'll Be Sorry' was written by Louis Armstrong himself. The version heard on the CD and cassette *Get Into Jazz* was recorded in Los Angeles in 1959 and features the great 'Satchmo' singing and playing a blistering trumpet solo. Trummy Young is on trombone, Peanuts Hucko on clarinet, Billy Kyle on piano, with Mort Herbert and Danny Barcelona playing bass and drums respectively. The piece is a good example of Dixieland music as developed by musicians in the Twenties and early Thirties in New Orleans and Chicago.

Louis Armstrong was one of the most influential musicians in the whole history of jazz and this song provides a fine example of his unique vocal delivery and his 'scat' singing (*see* pp. 29-30). After the sung verses and chorus, Armstrong directs Trummy Young to provide a short solo break into the final improvised instrumental section, where Armstrong himself takes his own solo to close the piece in typically fine form. Whether the lyrics of the song are autobiographical is uncertain and a closer look at his biography in Chapter Four may help you to make your own mind up.

Other great Dixieland bands to listen for are Kid Ory's Creole Jazz Band, Jack Teagarden's Sextet, The Original Dixieland Jazz Band and any band fronted by Ken Colyer, while other British bands such as those led by Acker Bilk, Kenny Ball and Chris Barber are all also well worth hearing.

The Louis Armstrong Story
Deja Vu: DVRECD 04 (CD)

Mahogany Hall Stomp
Living Era: ZCAJA 5049 (CD)

Satchmo's Greatest Hits
BMG: CX 89799 (LP/cassette)

BLUES/BOOGIE WOOGIE

'Ooh Boogie' (written by Sidney Bechet) performed by Sidney Bechet and his French Band

From one of the jazz world's most colourful characters, Sidney Bechet, we hear the wonderful 'bluesy' boogie woogie tune 'Ooh Boogie'. It was written by Bechet himself and was recorded on 5 November 1949; it features the great Kenny Clarke on drums (he later went on to become the 'creator of percussion bop') as well as Eddie Bernard on piano and Pierre Michelot on bass.

Bechet's sound on the soprano saxophone was unique. His distinctive heavy use of vibrato created an intensity to the sound that has inspired many who followed him. The track starts with the archetypal blues riff over a heavy walking bass line to the accompaniment of bluesy piano interjections. Perhaps now is a good time to clarify exactly what a 'riff' is, as the term is used widely in the context of jazz: a 'riff' is a short sequence of notes that is used many times in a piece – it may form an essential rhythmic device used in the accompaniment (as in this case) or even be the notes that go to make up the actual tune itself. The chord structure follows the traditional pattern of a twelve-bar sequence. Bechet takes an improvised solo in the second section of the tune and then hands over to Pierre Michelot who demonstrates his skill on the solo bass. The track closes with Bechet playing the opening statement once more, this time just slightly more impassioned.

This is a fine example of Sidney Bechet's sound and style. He was one of the most popular figures in the entertainment world in the postwar years, being a complete all-rounder, equally at home in a jazz club or on the Vaudeville stage.

RECOMMENDED LISTENING

Bluebird Sessions 1932-43
BMG Bluebird: ND 90317 (CD)

Platinum For . . .
Vogue: VGCD 600 026 (CD)

Sidney Bechet and Friends
Verve: 840 633-2 (CD)

SWING & BIG BAND

'*Don't Be That Way*' (written by Mitchell Parish,
Benny Goodman and Edgar Sampson)
performed by The Benny Goodman Band

Benny Goodman co-wrote the tune 'Don't Be That Way'
with two other very talented musicians, Mitchell Parish
and Edgar Sampson. Parish is also well known for his
work as a lyricist, collaborating with Hoagy Carmichael
among others, while Edgar Sampson was undoubtedly one
of the finest arranger/composers working in the swing
band era. Sampson was also a proficient saxophonist and
perhaps his biggest contribution to this track is the
excellent use of the sax section in the band with its
punctuating rhythm and subtle background sonorities.

From 'The King of Swing', Benny Goodman, the track
'Don't Be That Way' is a fine example of swing band
music that became so popular in the Thirties and the tune
is really very catchy. In true Goodman fashion, the
tune is embellished with great skill and dexterity by the
bandleader's impeccable clarinet playing. It's interesting
to hear how the rhythm section of bass and drums keeps
the tune driving along, with the bass providing a 'walking
line' and the drums giving the track a lift whenever it's
required. 'Walking' bass lines are commonly featured in
swing music, in particular, and provide a sound foundation for the tune that features on top – such bass lines
adhere very closely to the beat and rarely diverge from
the main pulse of the piece. There is also a great use of
light and shade in this piece, another feature typical of
the best tracks of this period. Glenn Miller employed the

same device – taking the band down from a healthy fortissimo to a whispering level, only for the audience to be startled by a cracking drum break to take the tune out on a rousing high note, which invariably left the audience shouting for more. The music was great for dancing, as well as just for listening, and numerous bands emerged at this time, among the most famous those of Benny Goodman, the Dorsey Brothers and Glenn Miller, while the big bands of Count Basie and Duke Ellington presented a style of music that was similar but more acceptable to the true jazz aficionados. The format of each of these bands would include a standard rhythm section of piano, bass and drums (sometimes with guitar), coupled with a small reed section (featuring alto, tenor and baritone saxes, with some players also playing flute and clarinets as required) and a brass section incorporating trumpets and trombones.

'Don't Be That Way' is one of those tunes that many will recognize even if they do not know the title. It was featured in nearly all of Benny Goodman's live concerts, among them the legendary 1938 Carnegie Hall concert, which was recorded and has become something of a landmark in the history of jazz, setting a precedent for jazz concerts to be staged at major concert halls and venues normally associated with classical music events.

Other fine examples of tunes from this era are Duke Ellington's 'Take The "A" Train', Count Basie's 'One O'Clock Jump' (*see Get Into Jazz* – the CD or cassette) and Glenn Miller's 'In The Mood'.

B. G. in Hi-Fi
Capitol: CDP 7926842 (CD)

Benny Rides Again
MCA: 31264 (CD)

Compact Jazz: Benny Goodman
Verve: 820543-2 (CD)

'Take The "A" Train' (written by Billy Strayhorn) performed by The Duke Ellington Band

'Take The "A" Train' was the Duke Ellington Band's signature tune. It was written by Billy Strayhorn, who many said was Ellington's alter ego. He was a very close friend of the Duke, one of his finest arrangers and an occasional pianist with the band. The version heard here on *Get Into Jazz* was recorded in June 1957 in New York and features the singer Ella Fitzgerald.

This recording is typical of the true Ellington sound – a beautifully schooled, tight, rhythm section that never stops swinging from the first note to the last and features the outstanding brass and saxophone sections. Ellington prided himself on having some of the most talented individuals in his band and he had a great gift for getting everyone to work well together. The band features such luminaries as Johnny Hodges on alto saxophone, Clark Terry and Dizzy Gillespie on trumpet and the legendary baritone saxophonist Harry Carney.

The tune opens with the most ingenious introduction, which, after the initial piano and rhythm section riffs, presents the reed section sounding like a train whistle – quite remarkable arranging. Ella Fitzgerald sings in fine form over subtle orchestrations provided by the band, who are not merely accompanying but playing a series of identifiable melodic lines. Ella improvises in a truly unique style of scat singing (her characteristic trade mark) and then we hear a set of solos from the virtuosi in the band, including the unmistakable sound of Dizzy Gillespie on trumpet. All the while, Duke Ellington is providing little riffs on the piano but very much taking a back seat while the pyrotechnics are taken care of by his trumpeters. The track takes another leap forward when the brass and reed sections play a set of fanfares to introduce the reappearance of the singer, who then weaves her way around the tune and presents the final version of the first verse, to take the track to the end of the line with the sound of the train whistles.

RECOMMENDED LISTENING

Black, Brown and Beige
RCA: PD 86641 (3CDs/4 cassettes)

The Complete Duke Ellington Volumes 1–5
CBS: 462985/6/7/8/9 (CDs/cassettes)

Duke Ellington and Friends
Verve: 833 291-2 (CD)

'One O'Clock Jump' (written by Count Basie) performed by The Count Basie Band

Count Basie had been a bandleader for some twenty years when this track was recorded. He is naturally often linked and compared with the other great band leader of the time, Duke Ellington, but invariably receives less praise from the established jazz critics. However, don't be put off – his music has such quality that it has stood the test of time, remains popular to this day and stands at the very pinnacle of big band jazz.

'One O'Clock Jump' was written by Count Basie himself and arranged by Ernie Wilkins. The version of this tune on the CD and cassette *Get Into Jazz*, was recorded on 27 June 1956 in New York and featured one of Basie's finest line-ups including The Count on piano and the recently hired Thad Jones on trumpet, Benny Powell and Henry Coker on trombones, Frank Foster and Frank Wess on saxes, all playing alongside the trusty rhythm section of Freddie Green, Eddie Jones and Sonny Payne. The tune is a prime example of a standard big band arrangement and was one of Count Basie's most popular numbers. Following the bluesy solo piano intro-duction (incorporating a riff that unquestionably was picked up later by Dave Brubeck to form the basis of his track 'It's A Raggy Waltz') we hear the opening tune, again on the piano, after which the tenor sax takes the lead with an accompanying figuration played by the rest of the saxes and brass instruments, with the rhythm section driving along in the background. A trombone solo featuring Henry Coker follows and then gives way to the extended tenor sax improvisation. Each of the key sidemen takes a solo turn thereafter and the track has an infectious catchiness about it that has made it immensely popular. Basie creeps in for his characteristically 'tinkling' solo and the track continues to build to the end with exciting drum fills deftly provided by Basie's drummer Sonny Payne. The tune comes to a close with a truly rip-roaring finale.

'One O'Clock Jump' is a classic Ernie Wilkins arrangement of what is arguably Count Basie's best-known tune.

Recommended Listening

The Atomic Mr Basie
Roulette: CDP 7932732 (CD)

Compact Jazz: Count Basie
Verve: 831364-2 (CD)

The Original American Decca Recordings 1937–39
MCA: GRP 36112 (3CDs/3 cassettes)

'CLASSIC' STANDARDS

'Summertime' (written by George Gershwin with lyrics/libretto by Edwin du Bose Heyward and Ira Gershwin) performed by Ella Fitzgerald and Louis Armstrong with an orchestra conducted by Russell Garcia

Choosing just a couple of standards to be included on the CD and cassette, I thought would be an impossible task. There are so many wonderful tunes and so many excellent versions of these tunes it seemed difficult to know where to start. However, when I was introduced to the song 'Summertime' as performed here, the problem was immediately solved. 'Summertime' is by George Gershwin, who was one of the great pioneers in introducing elements of jazz music into the classical music genre. He wrote the song as part of his opera *Porgy and Bess*, which was first performed in 1935, and it has since been sung (and played as an instrumental tune) by countless performers all over the world in every style of music imaginable. It is now regarded as one of his best-known and best-loved works.

Ella Fitzgerald and Louis Armstrong are, for me, the two artists best suited to this song – they have a natural feel for this type of music and the quality of their voices is so distinctive and evocative that it's no wonder this version has sold in huge numbers. They are two of the very biggest names in jazz and occasionally joined forces for concerts and recordings. This recording was made in September 1957 during a series of sessions that took place in Los Angeles throughout a thirteen-month period, with the two artists performing to the accompaniment of a scratch Hollywood Orchestra conducted by Russell Garcia. The contrast in style of the two singers adds to the end result with Ella Fitzgerald's smooth, jazzy vocal production starkly contrasting with Armstrong's gravelly, but immensely colourful delivery. A number of highly trained classical singers also like to sing this song but, in my opinion, the results are never very satisfactory because of their lack of real empathy with the music. If ever there was a good example of a 'classic standard', this version is it.

The track opens with a haunting introduction played by the full orchestra and Louis Armstrong bursts in on the trumpet with a laid-back but impassioned statement of this familiar tune. Ella Fitzgerald takes the next verse and from the moment she starts singing one is immediately drawn in to the mood of the song. Armstrong joins for the next verse and his unmistakable style beautifully complements Ella's next entry as he accompanies her with his 'scat' singing until the song eventually winds down to a close. One of the classic jazz recordings of all time.

RECOMMENDED LISTENING

Compact Jazz: Ella Fitzgerald Live
Verve: 833 294-2 (CD)

Compact Jazz: Ella Fitzgerald and Louis Armstrong
Verve: 835 313-2 (CD)

Porgy and Bess
Verve: 827475-2 (CD)

'April in Paris' (written by Vernon Duke E. Y. 'Yip' Harburg) performed by Billie Holiday

'April in Paris' is another very popular tune that has been performed by countless artists in as many styles in the last thirty years. Billie Holiday's version heard on this recording holds a special place in my CD collection, simply because it is one of the most haunting interpretations of the song that I've come across and the quality of Holiday's voice seems so evocative.

Considered by many as one of the best jazz vocalists of all time, Billie Holiday is heard here to the accompaniment of an illustrious collection of instrumentalists, including Ben Webster on tenor saxophone, Harry 'Sweets' Edison on trumpet, Jimmy Rowes on piano, Barney Kessel on electric guitar, Red Mitchell on bass and Alvin Stoller on drums. With such a line-up, it would be hard for this to be anything less than a completely captivating performance.

Billie Holiday had a unique talent – she could not read music and simply sang from the heart, with such feeling and intuition that she stands out as one of the true natural jazz legends. Some jazz critics have said that her voice lacks real quality – but what she lacked in beauty of timbre she certainly made up for with innate musical sensitivity and the ability to turn a phrase. What is particularly remarkable about Billie Holiday's artistry is the way that, even though her repertoire of songs was somewhat limited, every performance of even the most familiar of songs would contain something new in terms of nuance or phrasing, and this makes her a fascinating study for any enthusiast.

This recording was made just three years before her untimely death in 1959 and is a good example of her work during the Fifties. The band comprised many of her friends and this gives the recording a wonderful presence and intimacy which I find very engaging.

Recommended Listening

Compact Jazz: Billie Holiday
Verve: 831371-2 (CD)

Lady Day and Prez 1937-41 (with Lester Young)
Giants of Jazz: CD 53006 (CD)

The Legacy (1933-1958)
Columbia: 47724 (CD/cassette)

Bebop

'*Leap Frog*' (written by Charlie Parker)
performed by Dizzy Gillespie, Charlie Parker,
Thelonious Monk, Curly Russell and Buddy Rich

Bebop music originated during the immediate postwar period in the Forties and was a movement created by the black musicians of the day who wanted to move away from the commercial swing and big band sound, thereby extending the range of expression in their music. The music became extremely complex and often frenetic in feel, which aptly conveyed the mood of the time. Charlie

Parker, Dizzy Gillespie and Thelonious Monk (one of the co-writers of "Round Midnight') were among the most eminent of bebop musicians at the time and the track 'Leap Frog' by Charlie Parker is a perfect example of music from this period, featuring each of the three mentioned artists in particularly spectacular form. Naturally the white musicians of the day also became closely involved in developing the genre and on this particular recording we hear the drummer Buddy Rich playing in place of Max Roach who was the regular drummer in Charlie Parker's Quintet between 1947 and 1949.

'Leap Frog' is one of the most extraordinary tracks from the bebop era, demonstrating not only the phenomenal energy that this music can have, but also the astonishing virtuosity of the performers. In the version heard on *Get Into Jazz* we hear the two soloists Dizzy Gillespie and Charlie Parker in fine form – the rhythm section features the legendary Thelonious Monk on piano, Curley Russell on bass and the inimitable Buddy Rich on drums. Although this track takes less than three minutes to play, it gives an excellent insight into the world of bebop jazz.

Following the opening drum break, Charlie Parker leaps into a blistering alto sax solo which is answered by Gillespie on trumpet. This is followed by an exchange of musical dialogue between the two which is developed to a feverish pitch. Buddy Rich, one of the finest jazz/ big band drummers, steps in to break up the 'dog-fight' and towards the end of this track, his last drum solos are among the most marvellous examples of the great drummer at work. It's well worth noting the classic bebop hallmarks of this type of music – the driving rhythm from the bass alongside the open hi-hats in the drums, accompanied by the exotic chord punctuations from the piano, which provide the basis on which the soloists build and exchange their solos.

Many musicians playing bebop music (or bop as it is also known) were frequently under the influence of narcotics and this may well have contributed to the angst and manic quality of their music. Sadly, Charlie Parker was one such musician and died tragically early at the age of thirty-five, having lived life to the full but taken his drug habit just one stage too far.

RECOMMENDED LISTENING

Bird on Verve Volume 1
Verve: 817 442-1 (CD/LP)

Charlie Parker on Dial: Volumes 4 and 5
Spotlite SPJ: 104 and 105 (LP only)

Dizzy's Diamonds
Verve: 513 875-2 (CD)

COOL JAZZ

'Round Midnight (written by Thelonious Monk,
Bernie Hanighen and Cootie Williams, arranged
by Michel Legrand) performed by Miles Davis
with a band conducted by Michel Legrand

Recorded just eight months prior to John Coltrane's
'Grand Central' discussed below, ' 'Round Midnight' was
one of the tracks that came out of a series of sessions that
took place in New York on 25 June 1958, featuring the
arrangements of Michel Legrand. The tune was co-
written by Thelonious Monk, Bernie Hanighen and
Cootie Williams and has become one of the most commonly performed jazz tunes of all time.

As the profile in Chapter Four shows, Miles Davis was
a musical chameleon who had the ability to change with
the times – not for commercial reasons (although this must
have been a consideration) but rather in that he was able
to assimilate elements of many different styles of music
and produce his own hybrid sound, invariably with
magical results.

In the late Fifties, Miles Davis was playing with a
number of groups and for the sessions from which this
recording of ' 'Round Midnight' is taken, the line-up
reads like a *Who's Who of Jazz*: Michel Legrand, con-
ductor/arranger; Herbie Mann, flute; Betty Glamann,
harp; Barry Galbraith, guitar; John Coltrane, tenor saxophone; Phil Woods, alto saxophone; Jerome Richardson,
baritone saxophone; Eddie Costa, vibes; Bill Evans, piano;
Paul Chambers, bass; Kenny Dennis, drums and, of
course, Miles Davis on trumpet.

Michel Legrand provides a sensuous, exotic orchestral arrangement for Miles Davis to use as a backdrop for one of his best performances from these sessions. This recording is extremely evocative, sounding at times like a soundtrack from a movie, and the combination of the beautiful sounds emanating from the harp, vibes, guitar and flutes creates a texture that gives Miles not only just the right amount of space in which to extemporize, but also a wonderful palette of sound colours over which he plays in characteristically enigmatic form. It's an unusual recording – such exotic arrangements were not normally associated with the work of Miles Davis, but this track serves as a particularly interesting example of the great man on superlative form, producing the legendary sound of his muted trumpet.

RECOMMENDED LISTENING

Birth of the Cool
Capitol: CDP 792862 (CD)

Kind of Blue
CBS: 32109 (CD/cassette)

Porgy and Bess
CBS: 450 985 (CD)

HARD BOP

'Grand Central' (written by John Coltrane)
performed by John Coltrane (tenor saxophone),
Julian 'Cannonball' Adderley (alto saxophone),
Wynton Kelly (piano), Paul Chambers (bass) and
Jimmy Cobb (drums)

John Coltrane wrote the tune 'Grand Central' in the late Fifties and went to Universal Recording Studios in Chicago on 3 February 1959 to record a set of tracks with the alto saxophonist Julian 'Cannonball' Adderley. The rest of the band included Wynton Kelly, Paul Chambers and Jimmy Cobb.

Jazz in the late Fifties was in a state of change: Charlie Parker had been the predominant influence and innovator during the previous decade and, with the emergence of 'new' talents like Miles Davis, Thelonious Monk and Charlie Mingus, came new directions. The Miles Davis group of 1958–9 included both Adderley and Coltrane: Adderley was hailed as Charlie Parker's natural and deserving successor while Coltrane was even more complex in his expression and a true visionary in his approach.

The music presented here clearly demonstrates the distinctions between Adderley and Coltrane and gives us an insight into the music of the late Fifties in the immediate late-bop/pre-cool era. 'Grand Central' is an appealing track with wonderful ensemble playing from the two lead saxophonists as well as impeccable solo contributions. Coltrane's recorded legacy makes an interesting study and Julian 'Cannonball' Adderley can be heard on numerous recordings with such artists as Miles Davis, Bill Evans and Joe Zawinul.

RECOMMENDED LISTENING

John Coltrane Collection
Deja Vu: DVCD 2037 (CD)

A Love Supreme
MCA: DMCL 1648 (CD/LP/cassette)

My Favorite Things
WEA: K781 246-2 (CD)

LATIN JAZZ

'*Desafinado*' (written by Jobim/Mendonca)
performed by Stan Getz and Joao Gilberto with
Antonio Carlos Jobim, Tommy Williams, Milton
Banana and Astrud Gilberto

The tune 'Desafinado' is one that most people will immediately recognize and is very much in the same style as another familiar tune from this era, 'The Girl From Ipanema'. In the mid-Forties it started to be fashionable to incorporate Latin influences in jazz music; by the late Fifties it was extremely popular and an unqualified commercial success for the record companies who were bringing this kind of music to the attention of a wider public. The elements of Latin Jazz, however, really began to emerge in the Thirties and Forties and there have since been innumerable local variations in style. As early as the 1920s Afro-Cubop started the trend and artists like the Puerto Rican Juan Tizol (Duke Ellington's valve trombonist) wrote such tunes as 'Caravan', 'Conga Brava' and 'Perdido', which are probably the first examples of music in this genre.

Joao Gilberto was one of the most important musicians to appear on this scene and, with his wife, the singer Astrud Gilberto, he made a number of albums which are all well worth listening to. Stan Getz, the tenor saxophonist, was invited to record with the husband and wife duo and the result was *The Girl From Ipanema* album, which also features the track 'Desafinado' and others. Joao and Astrud are both excellent singers in this kind of material and the sparse, rhythmic accompaniment of the guitar and the Latin percussion sounds paint a wonderfully romantic and evocative picture. Stan Getz produces a very cool and husky sound on the tenor saxophone and is obviously very comfortable playing in this style. Getz never plays too many notes – the economy of expression is one of the main factors that gives the track its lazy, carefree atmosphere, making it ideal late-night or background listening. This easy, cool-sounding music is extremely evocative and there is an interesting catalogue of material to explore, featuring such artists as Joao Gilberto, Airto Moreira, Johnny Alf, Hermeto Pascoal and the exceptionally talented Antonio Carlos 'Tom' Jobim, who wrote the very popular tune 'Wave'.

Bossa Nova Jubilee Volumes 1 and 2
Tropical Music: 68.915 and 68.925 (CD)

Getz And Gilberto (Stan Getz and Joao Gilberto)
Verve: 810048-2 (CD)

Struck by Lightning (Airto Moreira and Flora Purim)
Virgin: CDVE 44 (CD)

MODERN JAZZ
'Take Five' (written by Paul Desmond)
performed by The Dave Brubeck Quartet

Mention the word jazz to many people, ask for the titles
of a few examples of famous tunes and 'Take Five' will
undoubtedly be near the top of most people's lists. It was
written in 1959 by Paul Desmond (not Dave Brubeck as
many imagine), who was the distinctive alto saxophonist
in the Dave Brubeck Quartet and is now regarded as one
of the most talented saxophonists of the twentieth century.

The tune was written for the repertoire of the Dave
Brubeck Quartet and has since been championed by
numerous jazz musicians from all backgrounds. What is
particularly unusual about the track is that it is in 5/4
time, i.e. five beats to the bar. Before this piece nearly all
jazz tunes were in two or four beats to the bar and this
'extra beat' was a radical departure from the norm.
Following its huge success, Dave Brubeck and Paul

Desmond followed 'Take Five' with a number of other tunes in unusual time signatures, like 'Blue Rondo A La Turk' and 'Take Ten'. The time signature was one of the reasons why 'Take Five' appealed so strongly to the first audiences who heard it: students from the university and college scene, where Brubeck's band toured during the Fifties. This predominantly young audience loved the curious intellectual challenge that such rhythmic devices presented; these days, the tune is appreciated purely on its own merits and has become very much a standard piece of repertoire.

Dave Brubeck's quartet made this tune an all-time favourite for many and there are dozens of live concert versions available. Quite often, these performances take not five, but closer to ten minutes because of the extended improvisations of Messrs Desmond and Brubeck – and the rest of the band when they could get a look in! This tune bears the hallmarks of the sound of Dave Brubeck's Quartet and his whole catalogue is worth listening to if this is your kind of jazz. The Modern Jazz Quartet has, not surprisingly, also recorded it in a similar 'modern jazz' vein and the pianist Oscar Peterson was the supreme master of this style of virtuoso, highly cultured, jazz piano improvisation.

The performance heard on the CD and cassette *Get Into Jazz* is taken from a concert given at the Interlochen Arts Academy in Michigan on 10 March 1976, in celebration of the Dave Brubeck Quartet's twenty-fifth anniversary.

25th Anniversary Reunion
A&M: 396998-2 (CD)

Take . . . The Greatest Hits
Elite: 009CD (CD)

Time Out
CBS: 62068 (CD)

'Stella by Starlight'
(written by Victor Young and Ned Washington)
performed by The Oscar Peterson Trio

Written by Victor Young and Ned Washington, the tune 'Stella by Starlight' is a well-known standard in the jazz repertoire. On this recording, which was made in Chicago on 4 May 1966, we hear the virtuoso pianist Oscar Peterson with Ray Brown and Louis Hayes on bass and drums respectively.

Oscar Peterson is regarded as one of the finest jazz pianists to have emerged in the last fifty years and he cites as two of his influences the great Teddy Wilson and Art Tatum (*see* Chapter Four for the latter). Peterson's playing encapsulates the finest traits of both these artists and combine with his own subtle qualities of musicianship to make him an artist that has that rare ability to appeal to a wide range of audiences.

'Stella by Starlight', as heard here, provides an insight into the master's art – at all times Peterson ensures that it's possible for the listener to keep in touch with the tune and the harmonies of the original version, but one is constantly fascinated by the exquisite, deft touches of virtuosity that sustain interest, as well as the sheer impact of such stunning technical brilliance. The accompaniment by the rest of the trio is in typical swing 'modern jazz' style, always moving, interesting and complementing the maestro at work.

RECOMMENDED LISTENING

Best of Oscar Peterson
Mercury: 830 698-2 (CD)

Compact Jazz: Oscar Peterson Plays Jazz Standards
Verve: 833283-2 (CD)

Night Train
Verve: 821724 (CD/LP/cassette)

ELECTRO-JAZZ-ROCK
'Captain Marvel' (written by Chick Corea) performed by Chick Corea and his band

Going a stage or two further from 'Desafinado' and the influences of the Latin countries (Brazil in particular), we hear Chick Corea's version of the tune 'Captain Marvel' which he wrote and recorded in London in 1972. This recording features a number of other influential musicians of this period including the bassist Stanley

Clarke, percussionist Airto Moreira (who was one of the pioneers of the Latin movement) and the vocalist Flora Purim – not forgetting the significant contribution made by Joe Farrell on flute.

Chick Corea is one of the current virtuoso keyboardists who was at the forefront of the jazz-rock fusion movement in the Seventies. He led a band called Return To Forever which presented music in the vein of 'Captain Marvel' with its Brazilian overtones and Latin influence. To me, the music also has deep roots in bebop and the energy expended in the improvised sections is very reminiscent of the earlier offerings of Charlie Parker and John Coltrane. Chick Corea managed, with considerable success, to combine all these elements with contemporary rock sounds into what became known as jazz-rock fusion and, although he has moved away from this style in recent years, jazz-rock fusion still has many ardent fans.

The tune 'Captain Marvel' is interesting for a number of reasons, not only because it features Corea, who had a major influence on the direction that jazz-based music was taking in the Seventies and Eighties, but because of the unusual cross-fusion of a number of different styles. From the minute the tune starts one is aware of the Brazilian influence with the Latin percussion sounds and light, almost be-bopian hi-hat cymbal playing, incessantly driving the tune along. Chick Corea immediately launches into a stunning display of technical virtuosity that many a bebop jazz musician would be proud of. Joe Farrell takes over with no less technical ability and we have the rather rare opportunity to sample a flautist extemporizing in a piece of jazz – an instrument that is not commonly used in this capacity. Flora Purim's background over-dubbed vocal lines in no way tax her quite exceptional ability, but add to the whole 'Seventies feel' of the track.

Other bands that were involved in this style of jazz at that time include Weather Report (featuring the saxophonist Wayne Shorter, keyboard virtuoso Joseph Zawinul, Peter Erskine on drums and the late but legendary Jaco Pastorius on bass guitar), Herbie Hancock and John McLaughlin's Mahavishnu Orchestra.

RECOMMENDED LISTENING

Bitches Brew
Columbia: 4606022 (CD)

Compact Jazz: Chick Corea
Polydor: 831 365-2 (CD)

Return To Forever
ECM: 8119782 (CD/LP)

CONTEMPORARY JAZZ

So many different strains of jazz are currently being presented and developed that, again, the choice was very difficult. For a number of reasons I have decided to include two tracks showing two different styles of jazz from the Nineties, both of which can be deemed 'accessible' on first hearing. It is tempting to include something extremely way-out and avant-garde but for the purposes of making a coherent album in its own right I have chosen the more mainstream contemporary jazz idioms as presented by two well-established and highly respected musicians, Paul Motian and Joe Henderson. Those whose interest lies in the more experimental side of jazz, I suspect, may have quite clearly defined preferences already (and probably are not in need of a guidebook like this) but those who do simply want to go right ahead and 'test-drive' some avant-garde jazz should proceed to Chapter Three and sample work by some of the names mentioned there.

Skylark (written by Johnny Mercer and Hoagy Carmichael) performed by the Paul Motian Band

Paul Motian has been around since the Fifties playing alongside many of the jazz greats including Bill Evans and Keith Jarrett. During the last twenty years he has led a number of bands (without piano) that have presented a wonderful mixture of standards and more contemporary styles of jazz. Leading the band from the drums (he is an absolute master of subtle jazz drumming using brushes), Motian has the ability to create a very special 'feel' to every track that is based on the rhythm section. 'Skylark' as heard here is no exception – it is a wonderful version of the Johnny Mercer/Hoagy Carmichael song and features Lee Konitz on soprano saxophone, Joe Lovano on tenor saxophone, Bill Frisell on guitar and Charlie Haden on bass. The result is a unique arrangement that gives ample space for the saxophonists to meander their way through the track to the accompaniment of some truly delightful guitar playing.

This is laid-back jazz and many will find enjoyment

here – the whole sound of the track is very easy on the ear, while never being boring, predictable or banal as much 'late night/background' jazz music tends to be.

RECOMMENDED LISTENING

Jack of Clubs
Soul Note: SN 1124 (CD)

Live in Tokyo
JMT/Phonogram: 8491542 (CD)

Paul Motian Plays Bill Evans
JMT: 834445 (CD/LP/cassette)

'Miles Ahead'
(written by Miles Davis and Gil Evans)
performed by Joe Henderson (tenor saxophone),
John Scofield (guitar), Dave Holland (bass) and Al
Foster (drums)

'Miles Ahead' was written by Miles Davis and Gil Evans back in the late Fifties and the version presented here is not in any way a re-creation of the original tune – the original version was arranged and conducted by Gil Evans for a nineteen-piece orchestra and so this arrangement for quartet bears little resemblance to the original.

Every few years a jazz album is released that brings together an exceptionally talented group of players who obviously have the same ideas about the music they are performing so that the results immediately communicate something very special to the listener. The album *So Near, So Far* is one such album; it was brought out in the spring of 1993 and features a quartet of some of the finest jazz musicians of recent years. The idea behind the album is simply to pay tribute to Miles Davis, whom all the performers agree had the most profound effect on their musical development. Miles Davis wrote all but one of the tracks on the album and the one featured here, 'Miles Ahead', dating from May, 1957, is probably the most famous.

The track starts in such a mellow way that we are immediately transported back in time to the very 'coolest' period of Miles Davis's career, featuring the economy of expression that was his hallmark. Joe Henderson had the honour of playing alongside Miles for a period in 1967 and it is an experience that he will never forget; the guitarist John Scofield also partnered Miles in the Eighties through four albums. Dave Holland played for three years in the late Sixties in the Miles Davis Band while Al Foster was undoubtedly the closest to the man, having been with him for over ten years. The effect of these associations is quite clear in the music and any serious study of Miles Davis's music will bear out what a very poignant and fitting tribute this recording is, drawing inspiration from the essential elements of the trumpeter's unique voice in the world of jazz. In his sleeve note on the record, Joe Henderson describes his feelings for Miles Davis and touches upon the extraordinary influence this great musician had on the whole jazz movement.

This track represents one side of what is going on in the jazz world today. It is a piece of music that has been created as a result of music that was written over forty years previously, and what makes this a truly fascinating and absorbing album is the way that these musicians have managed to create something entirely new out of this music from the past, in a context that is contemporary in feel and relevant to today's jazz audience, while still retaining its true spirit.

RECOMMENDED LISTENING

Dave Holland and Sam Rivers
Harmonia Mundi: 1238432 (CD)

Meant To Be (John Scofield)
Blue Note: CDP 795479-2 (CD/cassette)

So Near So Far (Joe Henderson)
Verve: 314 517 674-2 (CD)

CHAPTER THREE

The Last Decade and What's Happening Now?

When one looks at the Festival brochures and the gig lists sent out by today's jazz pubs and clubs, the first thing one notices is the incredible amount of jazz on offer today – it is exceedingly hard to know where to begin on a chapter like this. The second striking thing is the very wide cross-section of musicians – some are household names, while others are unknowns who may well never be heard of again.

However, one has to start somewhere and since it is impossible to include everyone who has made a significant contribution to the jazz movement over the last ten years or so, I have simply provided short outline profiles of a selected group of 'better-known' (I use the term quite loosely) artists who are currently active on the live circuit and/or have made recordings that you will be able to find in the jazz department of any major record store. This will both help you to widen your knowledge and assist you in your purchases. My apologies to those who are not featured here – there is bound to be controversy over who is deemed worthy of inclusion, but I've tried to put together a collection of musicians whose work is widely respected in all quarters, along with a number of artists whose work has given me enormous personal pleasure over the years. There seems little point in my recommending artists who have never made any recordings and are never likely to spread their wings further than, say, a small pub in South London, however phenomenally talented and interesting. Sadly, in the world of jazz, there are countless talented musicians who will never reach a wide public because of the very nature of the medium and the industry in which we work. I've therefore concentrated my efforts here on people, and their music, who are accessible to a wide public. Let's hope that those many talented musicians who are unknown at this time may find a way forward through the complexities of the record industry and live performance circuits, to the wider recognition they deserve.

In the late Seventies and early Eighties there were many different styles of jazz being presented, but the major record companies were predominantly releasing offerings focusing on electro-jazz and jazz fusion (in addition to albums from previously established artists and re-issues of back catalogue). Throughout Europe in the late Seventies, however, a number of independent record labels were set up to promote the talents of the many jazz musicians whose influences took in the folk music of cultures from all around the world; in the course of this chapter we will take a look at a number of these artists and bands.

If we start with the electro, funk and fusion-influenced players first, one band which just gets into 'the last decade' is Weather Report, a band that was the brainchild of saxophonist **Wayne Shorter** and the keyboard virtuoso and composer **Joe Zawinul**. Weather Report (so named because the band's style changed as often as the weather) played and recorded (with varying changes of personnel, but always retaining these two founder members) during a fifteen-year period which ended in 1985. They produced much very good and stimulating work, particularly on the best-selling album *Heavy Weather* which also featured one of the key sidemen-bass guitarist, the late Jaco Pastorius. Take a look at the entry on Joe Zawinul for some suggestions for recordings to listen to, but don't overlook his compatriot, the saxophonist Wayne Shorter, another remarkable musician whose work deserves to reach a wider public than the rather esoteric circuit of the jazz world.

Steps Ahead and the **Brecker Brothers** band are two outfits that have produced numerous excellent recordings (*see* the albums *Steps Ahead* of 1983, *Modern Times* of 1985 and *The Brecker Brothers*) and also still feature at the major jazz festivals. Michael Brecker is regarded as one of the finest tenor saxophonists of the present day, while brother Randy is a very gifted trumpeter indeed. Both brothers have experimented, with some degree of success, in using electronic devices to alter the sounds of their instruments and their own band has been acclaimed as probably the finest fusion band around.

Herbie Hancock and **Chick Corea** have continued to

65

develop from where they left off in the late Seventies. Hancock, who made a slight diversion in the early Eighties into the field of acoustic music, is now firmly back on the path of electronic exploration. Chick Corea is regarded, alongside Keith Jarrett, as one of the most significant solo pianists on the scene and he has also ventured into the classical music field, producing some fascinating results. Corea's and Hancock's musical associates of some fifteen years ago are also still actively involved in the contemporary jazz scene, both as performers and, more commonly, as soloists on albums made in the United States. Artists who come into this category include people like the drummer **Steve Gadd** and the guitarist **Al DiMeola**, both of whom, one could legitimately argue, really deserve to be in the Giants of Jazz section. Their music is definitely worthy of exploration and they (and others from this era) can be heard on all manner of jazz and pop records as soloists, appearing almost incognito – check your favourite album sleeves and their names will surely appear.

Moving on to some guitarists, **John McLaughlin** and **Pat Metheny** still have very wide followings – both are extensively recorded and McLaughlin's Mahavishnu Orchestra (which he started with the drummer Billy Cobham) was a truly innovative ensemble that inspired many up-and-coming jazz bands and holds a very special place in the history book of jazz. Pat Metheny continues to have a very open and experimental attitude to his music making: he is an expert in guitar synth techniques and manages to combine many different styles into a unique and immediately identifiable sound that has very much become his own. Other guitarists worthy of mention here include **John Scofield** and **Bill Frisell**, both of whom have achieved widespread popularity. Scofield was a pupil at the Berklee School of Music and, in his early twenties, was enlisted to play alongside such all-time greats as Chet Baker, Gerry Mulligan and Gary Burton. He has since gone on to pursue both a solo career and active involvement with a number of band projects. Frisell is another ex-Berklee School student who has developed an eclectic style: he's often to be heard playing alongside the veteran drummer Paul Motian (of whom more later), Jan Garbarek, Carla Bley, Eberhard Weber and many others.

The Yorkshireman, **Allan Holdsworth**, (born 1946), was one of the first pioneers of jazz rock and fusion styles, heavily reliant on electronics. He joined the band Soft Machine in 1973 and also worked with Tony Williams, Bill Bruford, Jean-Luc Ponty and others, while pursuing a very individual solo career throughout the Eighties. He is an extraordinarily gifted virtuoso guitarist and, with the advanced use of electronics, has the ability to emulate the sound and characteristics of wind instruments to astonishing effect. The album *With A Heart In My Song* presents a good mixture of his work, featuring his MIDI controlled guitar on a number of tracks.

On the trumpet front in the last few years we have seen the sad loss of two of the greatest of all time in **Miles Davis** and **Dizzy Gillespie**. However, a number of very different styles of trumpet playing are still to be heard in the jazz scene, among them **Wynton Marsalis**, who was born in New Orleans in 1961 and has carved a unique position in the music industry as both a classical and a jazz trumpet virtuoso. After leaving the Juilliard School in New York, he joined Art Blakey's Jazz Messengers and also played in the quartet with Herbie Hancock, Ron Carter and Tony Williams as a 'replacement' for Miles Davis. An extremely exciting musician, Marsalis is not only able to play jazz and classical music with equal ease, he is also a fine stage performer who turns his hand to many different styles of jazz. Most recently seen at the London Prom Concerts in the Albert Hall, Marsalis was not giving a classical concert as one might expect in this series, but, with his septet, he treated the audience to a fine display of soulful New Orleans jazz!

Quite different but equally riveting is the blistering virtuoso talent of the Cuban trumpeter, **Arturo Sandoval**. Born in 1949, Sandoval is a phenomenally gifted all-round musician and showman – he formed the band Irakere in 1973, does tours and sell-out live concerts all over the world as a soloist, is frequently invited to guest with all sorts of bands and has made some superlative recordings. He can be seen in the film *A Night in Havana* playing alongside Dizzy Gillespie, but if you get the chance to see him live, don't miss it – he's one of the most entertaining jazz acts on the circuit today. The band Irakere is also (with or without Sandoval) a highly enjoyable band to see live. Full of high-spirited multi-instrumentalists, their exciting repertoire is presented in a true party atmosphere, ensuring them sell-out appearances at festivals and clubs everywhere.

Featured on the CD and cassette *Get Into Jazz*, the drummer **Paul Motian**, who was born in 1931, is another name from the past who is still very active and producing interesting work today. In his early days throughout the Fifties and Sixties he played a lot with people like Bill Evans, Zoot Sims and Charles Lloyd, forming a partnership some years later with Charlie Haden and Keith Jarrett. Since 1974, however, he has been fronting his own bands – the albums mentioned in Chapter Six, featuring arrangements of Broadway Songs (with Charlie Haden, Bill Frisell and Joe Lovano) are among my own personal favourites, while his work with the Electric Bebop Band has also produced some interesting results.

Among top-level saxophonists of the last ten or fifteen years, there are many who deserve special mention. The saxophone is still probably the single most popular instrument in jazz and it comes as no surprise that there is a plethora of highly talented individuals playing the saxophone in all styles – some harking back to the bebop and the post-bebop eras, others in effect creating new sounds and styles that are being copied and developed by the latest generation of saxophonists, who are in their early twenties. **Joe Henderson** is right at the top of the tree, playing better than ever before. Now in his late fifties, Henderson has developed from his earlier work with Horace Silver, Freddie Hubbard and Herbie Hancock, to present a style all of his own. He is a very fine improviser, never seeming short of new inspiration – his latest album *So Near, So Far* (on the Verve label) contains much of his finest work and is well worth exploring. From a completely different camp is the altogether more commercial player **David Sanborn**. Sanborn's background contains an interesting mixture of jazz, blues and pop influences – he had a long association with the wonderful jazz musician Gil Evans and, inspired by the likes of Charlie Parker and Hank Crawford and his deep love of the blues, has produced some extremely powerful music in the pop and rock fields as well. His hallmark is a vibrant, cutting sound that is charged with emotion and he has a virtuoso technique that enables him to play almost anything in any style. He occasionally (in addition to his commercial studio work) goes out with his own quartet, but is much in demand as a solo player.

Many fine saxophonists from the younger generation have emerged over the last ten years or so, some of whom have undoubtedly benefited from a significant degree of media hype – something relatively unheard of in the jazz world until recently. In the last two or three years, the marketing men have focused a good deal of attention on the image-creating process that was hitherto predominantly associated with the pop industry. However, it is widely accepted that a by-product of such hype has been the promotion of the whole jazz cause, and that can only be considered a positive step towards making jazz accessible to a wider audience.

From New Orleans and born in 1960, **Branford Marsalis**, (Wynton's brother), is one of the most successful saxophonists of the present day. His earlier work with the Herbie Hancock Quartet was much respected, bringing him to the attention of the pop star Sting, who brought Marsalis, pianist Kenny Kirkland and bass player Darryl Jones together to do a jazz/pop album entitled *Dream of the Blue Turtles*. Several British saxophonists are also currently enjoying successful careers; they include **Courtney Pine**, **Andy Sheppard** and **Tommy Smith**, all of whom were influenced principally by the playing of John Coltrane. Smith is perhaps the most diverse in his approach and has made one or two excellent recordings – he is the first British musician to have been signed as a 'leader' by the US-based Blue Note jazz label. His first album *Step by Step*, which also features the talents of John Scofield and Jack DeJohnette, has been very favourably received. Courtney Pine, the first British-born black musician to make a real impact on the UK jazz scene, is enjoying considerable success as a soloist; he originally made his mark playing with the John Stevens Freebop Band and Art Blakey's Jazz Messengers.

Of the 'middle' generation saxophonists, there are many players who have made it through the last twenty years or so and are still very active on the contemporary jazz circuit. Among these, I must mention a handful of musicians who have been the source of much inspiration and enjoyment to me personally, both at live concerts and on recordings. **Tony Coe** comes immediately to mind – talented and supremely inventive on clarinets and saxes equally, Coe is regarded as one of the most versatile of all jazz musicians from the UK. He started out playing in the mainstream jazz/big band circuit with leaders like Humphrey Lyttelton and John Dankworth and at one time was invited to join the Count Basie band. However, being a true individualist, Coe formed a number of groups of his own and presented a diverse range of material, from music of the bebop era and mainstream renditions of 'standards', to challenging contemporary jazz and avant-garde classical music. One of his most famous works (as a composer and a player) is the one commissioned by the Arts Council of Great Britain, *Zeitgeist*, which is scored for large forces, solo instrumentalists and vocalists and brings in the talents of collaborators like the clarinettist Alan Hacker, with whom Coe has worked closely in the past. One of my favourite examples of Coe's clarinet virtuosity is to be found in the track 'Rio Vermhilo' from the album *Coe-Existence*, while any album featuring Coe on saxes in undoubtedly well worth hearing.

Pete King is another player whose career I've followed quite closely – now in his mid-fifties and playing exceptionally, as ever. He started out, like Coe, playing in the big band scene, but his natural musical affinity is to the bebop sound and, to that end, his work in smaller groups is now regarded as his most successful. He is often to be found playing at the major jazz clubs and festivals and broadcasts regularly.

Two American saxophonists whose work is worthy of attention are **Steve Lacy** and **Yusef Lateef**, both well known on the international jazz festival circuit. Lacy's development as an artist has closely followed the historical changes of the last thirty or forty years. His earliest interest in New Orleans and Kansas City jazz moved on to an avid interest in the bebop school, of which he became a staunch disciple: indeed, he had the good fortune to play in the Thelonious Monk Quartet for some months in the late Fifties and this undoubtedly proved to be the most significant period in his career. Yusef Lateef was born in Chattanooga, Tennessee and moved to New York in his mid-twenties where he eventually joined the Dizzy Gillespie band, with whom he worked for just over a year. Later collaborations were with Charles Mingus and Julian 'Cannonball' Adderley. Lateef is regarded as a true all-rounder – he plays oboe and flute exceptionally well and has also been known to perform using a 7-Up bottle!

Widely recognized as one of the great saxophonists of the last thirty years is the American **Phil Woods**, whose track record reads like an entry in a *Who's Who of Jazz*. Among the major musicians in whose bands he has played are Dizzy Gillespie, Buddy Rich, Quincy Jones and Benny Goodman – but it is as a soloist that he has really made his mark. Woods has guested on numerous jazz albums and also crossed over into the pop world, perhaps his most famous and popular contribution being the solo on Billy Joel's chart-topping single 'Just The Way You Are'. Phil Woods formed his own quartet, the European Rhythm Machine, in the late Sixties and since that time has fronted a number of small combos, visiting many of the prestige jazz festivals and clubs around the world. His style is very much derived from the Parker school but retains his own unique characteristics of inflections in the tone and an immediately accessible sense of harmonic structure in his soloing. Phil Woods has been the source of inspiration for many of today's up-and-coming young jazz saxophonists.

In addition to Chick Corea and Herbie Hancock (*see* pp. 65, 119, 159), **Keith Jarrett** has made a huge impact in the last twenty years or so, particularly with his solo piano recordings for the German record company ECM, which has played such an important role in bring- ing contemporary jazz music to the public's attention. Manfred Eicher, who started the label, almost single- handedly set out to create a major competitor for the big American record companies who were focusing their energies on releasing jazz funk and fusion discs. Eicher signed up Keith Jarrett when his Columbia contract expired and other musicians like Gary Burton, The Art Ensemble of Chicago, Pat Metheny, John Abercrombie and Sam Rivers were among many who enjoyed a new sense of creative freedom on the ECM label. Jarrett's quartet with Jan Garbarek, Palle Danielsson and Jon Christensen was thought by many to be the finest small combo outfit throughout the Seventies and into the Eighties and their recordings are well worth exploring.

From Holland, where there is a very strong interest in modern jazz, **Willem Breuker** is an exciting talent. Breuker is a saxophonist/composer whose albums have received rave reviews from the majority of critics – the music is diverse and challenging, containing references to all kinds of styles, ranging from the music of George Gershwin and Duke Ellington to ethnic styles, music theatre and the avant-garde classicists. The album *To Remain* is well worth hearing but is difficult to obtain outside his native country.

The current interest in jazz is enabling numerous new and young talents to come forward and the scene is set to become even more interesting as the decade progresses and more festivals and venues thrive. The British keyboard player and founder of Loose Tubes, **Django Bates,** has recently been signed by Verve and we can expect some highly innovative material from him – look out for his new CDs from 1994. With the added assistance of forward-thinking record companies, like Verve and ECM, who are prepared to give artists the necessary degree of freedom, we shall undoubtedly see some very exciting and inspiring work from around the world.

CHAPTER FOUR

The Giants of Jazz: an A–Z

In this chapter we are going to look at the life and times of many of the greatest exponents of jazz to have emerged since its inception. In addition, I've included profiles on some other artists who have made their mark in the jazz field in the last twenty years or so without being truly innovative or influential in the way that people like Louis Armstrong or Charlie Parker were, but who, nevertheless, have made a significant contribution to the jazz movement as a whole. In every case, I have included a selection of recommended listening – this will assist you in your search for some of the best examples of each performer's work. So, whether your preferences lie in trad jazz performed by Acker Bilk and Kenny Ball, or in the music of the hard-core bebop artists like John Coltrane and Dizzy Gillespie, there is something here for everyone.

The instruments that have been used in jazz bands to the best effect are the saxophones, clarinet, piano, bass, drums, guitar, trumpet, trombone and vibraphone; outstanding artists on each of these are included in this chapter, as is a selection of the finest jazz vocalists and some other instrumentalists who have specialized in performing on instruments not normally associated with jazz. Before we begin on the profiles, it's worth clarifying the main differences between the members of the saxophone family, as the sound of each of these instruments is very distinctive. Most people will agree that the individual members of the saxophone family are the ideal instruments for playing jazz. The whole range of expressions and emotions can be produced and even the physical look and feel of these instruments are now almost synonymous with jazz. There are four main types: the soprano, alto, tenor and baritone, while both the soprano and baritone have smaller and larger brothers, respectively, in the sopranino and the bass. The saxes most commonly used as solo instruments in jazz are the alto and the tenor, while each of the other members is represented in sax sections in bands; there have also been some phenomenally gifted soloists on both the soprano and the baritone. All the major influential sax players are included in this chapter.

While it's impossible to include everyone who has been influential or highly acclaimed, here follows an insight into the lives and times of many of the finest jazz musicians ever to have graced the world's stages.

Julian 'Cannonball' Adderley (1928–75)
(alto sax, soprano sax)

Born into an exceptionally musical family, Julian Adderley studied a whole range of brass and reed instruments while at school. His father was a jazz cornet player but encouraged his son to specialize in the members of the saxophone family. Immediately on leaving high school Julian became involved in several bands in Florida, becoming the band director of the Dillard High School in 1948. During the early Fifties, while serving in the army, he directed and played in a number of jazz and dance bands.

Julian was a big man and was given the nickname 'Cannibal' by his high school colleagues who were ever amazed at his vast eating capacity. A chance mishearing by someone in the music business brought about the new name 'Cannonball' and he made his first break into the 'big time' when playing with Oscar Pettiford at the Bohemia in New York in the summer of 1955. A month or so later he was signed up by EmArcy Records and formed a quintet with his brother Nat, who was a gifted cornet and trumpet player. They made a fine recording in the album *Somethin' Else*, which featured a guest performance by Miles Davis, and Julian was invited to join the Miles Davis Band the following year.

After a two-year stint with Miles Davis, Adderley left the group to do a tour with George Shearing as the featured soloist and, later that year, re-formed the original quintet with his brother. This group went on to be one of the most successful jazz combos of the late Fifties and early Sixties. A number of celebrated jazz musicians passed through the band, including Weather Report keyboardist Joe Zawinul, the saxophone and reed player Yusef Lateef (when the band became a sextet); Charles Lloyd replaced Lateef and in 1965 George Duke took over from Zawinul.

Adderley's style was very reminiscent of his idol Charlie Parker and he also held Benny Carter in high regard. He had the agility and energy of Parker and the beauty of tone of Carter and these place him as one of the true greats among the jazz saxophonists of the last forty years. He died suddenly in Gary, Indiana of a heart attack but has left a marvellous legacy of very fine recordings, a number of which are currently available on CD.

RECOMMENDED LISTENING

Just Friends
Charly: CDCHARLY 58 (CD)

Know What I Mean?
Original Jazz Classics: OJC 105 (CD/LP/cassette)

Somethin' Else
Blue Note: CDP 7463382 (CD/cassette)

Talkin' About You
Landmark: LCD 1528 2 (CD)

Them Dirty Blues
Landmark: 1301 (CD/LP/cassette)

Louis Armstrong (1900–71)
(cornet, trumpet, vocals)

Louis Armstrong was born in Jane Alley in New Orleans and has become one of the best-known jazz musicians of all time. He traditionally gave his birth date as 4 July 1900, but it is quite likely that he was born at least a few years earlier and the change of date was made in order to avoid conscription for the First World War. He came from an impoverished background – his parents split up when he was just five years old and while being brought up solely by his mother, young Louis had to sing on the corners of streets to earn money to keep the family going. On the night of New Year's Eve, 1913, Louis was so carried away by the festivities that he celebrated the coming of the New Year by firing a pistol that he'd taken from his mother without her knowledge. He was promptly arrested and sent away to a Waifs' Home where he was given a cornet to play in the institution band. His interest in and love of music was at last being fulfilled and, capitalizing on the experience, on his release from the Waifs' Home in New Orleans, he took jobs with a variety of bands, including those of Kid Ory, Papa Celestin's Tuxedo Brass Band and Fate Marable's riverboats. In 1922 Armstrong left for Chicago and four years later he switched over to playing the trumpet, the much brighter-sounding instrument on which he was to become a world-famous performer.

He joined King Oliver's Creole Jazz Band at the Lincoln Gardens and although already married to Daisy Parker, a New Orleans 'hostess', he met and fell in love with Oliver's pianist, Lilian Hardin. Armstrong was very much a 'ladies man' and vividly recalls a number of his antics in his autobiography *My Life in New Orleans* (Da Capo Press, New York). The combination of his boyish charm and his unquestioned musical talent made him irresistible to the ladies. Lilian was a very talented lady who later had her own bands and quite soon after their first meeting it became obvious she was going to be the second Mrs Armstrong. They married in 1924 but Louis had to leave home the following year to go to New York where he had been invited to work with the Fletcher Henderson Band at the Roseland Ballroom. He travelled between New York and Chicago, as much to keep Lilian's suspicions of his possible infidelity at bay, and it was during this period that he really made a name for himself through the recordings issued as Louis Armstrong's Hot Five and Hot Seven. The first tune to be recorded was 'My Heart' and this set the ball rolling for a string of immensely popular releases that earned him a worldwide reputation. The band was exceptional, featuring some of the finest players around, including Earl 'Fatha' Hines on piano, Johnny Dodds on clarinet, Kid Ory on trombone and the drummers Zutty Singleton and 'Baby' Dodds.

As well as being one of the finest jazz trumpeters, he was a very expressive singer and a much respected bandleader. He fronted a band at Connie's Inn in Harlem and made his mark in shows like Hot Chocolates (in which he introduced the hit song 'Ain't Misbehavin' ', written especially for the show by the legendary pianist Fats Waller). Following the enormous success of 'Ain't Misbehavin' ', Armstrong led numerous big bands, presenting mainly popular tunes as his material. This didn't please the jazz purists but ensured his fame and fortune. However, such was the sincerity of the man, he never sold his soul to the commercial world. Everything he did was done with conviction and honesty. He toured throughout Europe in 1932, headlining a show at the London Palladium and in a feature in *Melody Maker*, the editor amusingly misquoted his nickname 'Satchelmouth' as 'Satchmo', and this was how he was known until his death.

Because of the incredible success of his recordings all around the world, Louis Armstrong became a huge media figure and was consistently on show as an all-round entertainer, yet again upsetting the jazz purists. He took part in more than thirty movies of varying quality and this too enlarged the number of his admirers. Thankfully for the real music lovers, Armstrong's dedication to jazz meant that playing the trumpet was his first love and he formed one of the all-time great bands of the late Forties, the Louis Armstrong 'All Stars' – and all stars they certainly were: Jack Teagarden on trombone, Barney Bigard on clarinet, Dick Cary on piano, Sid Catlett on drums and Arvell Shaw on bass. Together they made great music and Armstrong was in his prime at this time. The band toured all over the world to all the major venues and international festivals and the effect that Louis had on the whole jazz trumpet-playing world was enormous. Dizzy Gillespie is quoted as saying 'If it weren't for him, there wouldn't be any of us.' The tributes paid to him after his death were unanimous in their praise for a truly re-markable artist and human being. He was a loving, caring man who always brought out the best in everyone that he met and he was adored both by the public at large and by the whole of the music profession.

Armstrong derived great satisfaction and enjoyment from singing and always recognized that he could reach a much wider audience through singing than he could by playing the trumpet – the prime example of this was his single 'What A Wonderful World', which was a huge hit all over the world. He also enjoyed performing in large stadiums – he soon became accustomed to this when he was topping the bill as a singer. At about the age of sixty, Armstrong began to play less and less and certainly there are few recorded occasions when he showed his talent for improvising on the trumpet after the early 1960s.

Louis Armstrong suffered a severe heart attack in March 1971. He left hospital the following May and died peacefully, in his sleep, at home in New York on 6 July. Following his death at the age of seventy-one, Joachim Berendt is quoted as saying that 'without Louis Armstrong there would be no jazz – without jazz, there would be no modern popular music and no rock.' He went on to state that had it not been for Armstrong, jazz might have remained just a sort of folk music from New Orleans, with little world profile. While some may think this a slight over-reaction at a very sad moment in the history of jazz, he may well have been right.

It seems appropriate to end this section on the great Satchmo with a few words that he wrote – for me they encapsulate the whole spirit of the man: 'I fell in love with it (the trumpet) and it fell in love with me – what we play is life and a natural thing.'

Compact Jazz: Louis Armstrong
Verve: 833293-2 (CD)

Ella and Louis Again Volumes 1 and 2
Verve: 825373-2 and 82537484-2 (CD)

Hot Fives and Hot Sevens Volume 3
JSP: 314 (CD)

Louis Armstrong and Duke Ellington:
  The Complete Sessions
Roulette: CDP 793844-2 (CD)

Louis Armstrong and His Orchestra 1932–33
Classics: 529 (CD)

Louis in New York: Volume V
Columbia: CK 46148 (CD)

Satchmo
Pickwick: PWK 009 (CD)

What A Wonderful World
Bluebird: ND 88310 (CD)

Chet Baker (1929–88)
(trumpet, flugel, vocals)

Born in Oklahoma in 1929, Chet Baker was, at a very early stage, already tipped for the top by many in the jazz world. In fact, in 1950, Charlie Parker is quoted as saying to

Miles Davis 'You'd better watch out. There's a little white cat on the West Coast who's gonna eat you up!' However, despite a highly successful career, Chet Baker never did 'eat' Miles up but he did much good work with a host of other talented musicians in the Fifties and Sixties, playing alongside such artists as Gerry Mulligan, Russ Freeman and later Bill Evans.

His style was light and wistful – very 'cool' and laid back, in the true tradition of West Coast jazz. Some jazz critics have found fault with Baker's playing, commenting that he invariably sounds diffident and unsure of himself, while it is this understated playing which is found so appealing by many others – when one hears what blistering virtuoso lines he could play, such as those on the album *The Best of Chet Baker Plays*, such criticisms seem totally unwarranted.

One of my personal favourite collaborations was Chet Baker with the similarly laid-back alto saxophonist Paul Desmond, who is more closely associated, of course, with Dave Brubeck's band. A recent release of Baker and Desmond playing together in the Seventies makes for some wonderful listening, featuring classic performances of a number of old favourites – standards like 'Tangerine', 'I'm Getting Sentimental Over You' and 'Autumn Leaves'.

Baker had a terrible drug problem and was often in trouble. He got involved in a punch-up in San Francisco in 1968 which resulted in his losing his front teeth – every horn player's worst nightmare – which meant that he couldn't play for some time. However, by the mid-Seventies he was back in good form and playing as beautifully as ever. He came to an unsavoury end by falling out of a hotel window in Amsterdam, reputedly while under the influence of narcotics.

RECOMMENDED LISTENING

Chet Baker and Paul Desmond
Epic: 472984-2 (CD)

Chet Baker in Paris Volume 1
EmArcy: 837474-2 (CD)

Compact/Walkman Jazz: Chet Baker
Verve: 840630-2 (CD)

The Route (Chet Baker and Art Pepper)
EMI/Pacific Jazz: CDP 792931-2 (CD)

You Can't Go Home Again
A&M 396997 (CD)

Kenny Ball (born 1930)
(trumpet, vocals)

Kenny Ball started out in life as an electrician who took up the trumpet and did a few gigs as a semi-professional musician, finally becoming a fully fledged professional trumpeter in the mid-Fifties. His earliest appearances in the jazz world were with some highly talented bands, including those led by the trombonist Charlie Galbraith and drummer Eric Delaney. He later joined the prestigious band led by the clarinettist Sid

Phillips, where he earned a very high reputation indeed. In the late Fifties he left Sid's band to form his own group, which became an immediate success on the trad jazz scene and since the hit record featuring the Cole Porter tune 'Samantha' in 1961, Kenny Ball hasn't looked back. This record was followed later that year by 'Midnight in Moscow', which led to a string of TV and radio appearances in Britain and offers of live concert appearances throughout Europe.

Kenny Ball made his mark, first and foremost, as an outstanding trad jazz trumpeter, one of the very best in Britain. His qualities as a natural all-round entertainer developed throughout the Sixties but in the latter part of the decade the rise in popularity of pop and rock music took the spotlight away from bands like Kenny Ball's; the inevitable consequence was his move towards the cabaret scene and tours outside Britain. He made a number of personnel changes within the band, bringing in the clarinettist Andy Cooper and pianist Johnny Parker (later to be replaced by Hugh Ledigo), and the band continues to enjoy considerable success at home and abroad.

Kenny Ball's recorded output falls into two categories: that which appeals more to the mass market by way of its middle-of-the-road content and, of more interest to the band itself, the out-and-out trad jazz that they play with undoubted enthusiasm. Always an enjoyable band to watch, Ball has developed a loyal following and a style of presentation that works well both in concert halls and on TV. Appearances on shows like the Royal Variety Performance and with Morecambe and Wise in Britain ensured a wide audience that has stayed with the band to the present day.

Ball Plays British
MFP: CDMFP 6072 (CD)

The Collection
Castle Communications: CCSCD 258 (CD)

Golden Hour of Kenny Ball and His Jazzmen
Knight Records: KGHCD 131 (CD)

Have A Drink On Me
Pickwick: PWK 043 (CD)

On Stage
Start Records: STOCD 102 (CD)

Chris Barber (born 1930)
(trombone, bass trumpet, vocals)

Born in Welwyn Garden City in 1930, Chris Barber is recognized as one of the great pioneers of the British jazz scene. He is best known for being a very fine trombone player and bandleader but, surprisingly, started his musical studies as a violinist and soprano saxophonist. He was originally closely associated with the Ken Colyer Band in the mid-Fifties (a band that he subsequently took over in 1954) and later set up his own New Orleans-sounding band which he constantly developed in style and in the constantly varying combinations of instrumental line-ups. His biggest hit record was 'Petite Fleur' in 1959 which reached number three in the UK chart and number five in the United States.

'Petite Fleur' made a significant impact on the trad jazz boom in Britain during the late Fifties and undoubtedly helped pave the way for fellow Brits Kenny Ball and Acker Bilk, among others. Barber's band presented a wider repertoire, including a lot of blues music alongside the New Orleans trad for which he is particularly famous. His marriage to the blues singer Ottilie Patterson has fuelled this cross-over into the blues repertoire and really has widened the stylistic horizons of his band. He went on to work with a diverse collection of other singers both at home and in America, where he has established a fine reputation as a great jazz all-rounder.

He often teamed up with his friend and colleague Acker Bilk and released a couple of big-selling duet albums in the early Sixties, which were only superseded in the success stakes by the album *The Best of Ball, Barber and Bilk* when the marketing men also linked them up with Kenny Ball – a shrewd move and one that did much to promote the British cause in trad jazz.

RECOMMENDED LISTENING

The Entertainer (Chris Barber Jazz Band)
Polydor: 832593-2 (CD)

Essential Chris Barber
Kaz Records: KAZCD 13 (CD)

Jazz Band Favourites (Chris Barber Jazz Band)
EMI: CC 273 (CD)

The Ultimate
Kaz: KAZCD 4 (CD)

When It's Thursday Night In Egypt
Sonet: SNTCD 996 (CD)

Count Basie (1904–84)
(piano, organ)

Born William Basie in 1904 in New Jersey, 'Count' Basie made an early start in music, being taught to play the piano by his mother and later having lessons from the legendary 'Fats' Waller. He started out as a professional pianist playing the vaudeville cabaret circuit as part of the band known as The Blue Devils. The band broke up in the mid-Thirties and the majority of players moved to a new band led by Bennie Moten. However, when Moten died in 1935, Basie took over and immediately put the band on the map, both as a recording unit and as a live act which developed an enormous following very quickly. Like Duke Ellington, Basie surrounded himself with absolutely first-rate players and his band is immediately identifiable by the uncanny perfection of all the solos performed within the beautifully crafted arrangements.

The rumour goes that Count Basie got his suitably regal title from the impresario William Alexander who acted for Benny Goodman, 'The King of Swing'. With a King, 'Duke' Ellington and Earl 'Fatha' Hines, a Count was definitely needed! In 1936 his band went to New York and although unsuccessful at first, they achieved considerable popularity in the end. The early problems were partly due to the fact that many of the players, although supremely talented musicians, were not first-rate sight-readers and Basie's arrangements needed well-schooled players to make them work. This, coupled with the fact that not many of them could afford decent instruments, led to some mixed results in the initial stages. However, they eventually got things sorted out and when the band was engaged to open the new club, The Famous Door, it immediately made a big impact and was the talk of the town. Count Basie led the band from the piano with an elegant style (listen to his contribution on the track 'One O'Clock Jump', featured on the CD and cassette *Get Into Jazz*); he was a very gifted pianist who played with remarkable economy – no long solos or flashy pyro-technics, just pure talent, demonstrated in his somewhat minimalist solos.

Basie's bands naturally went through a number of personnel changes over the years but the Count was involved in the jazz and mainstream entertainment world right up to the time of his death in 1984. Although his band was always a fine instrumental ensemble in its own right, Basie invited a number of the world's leading vocalists to join him; these included such artists as Billy Eckstine, Tony Bennett, Ella Fitzgerald, Sarah Vaughan and Frank Sinatra.

Basie was undoubtedly one of the finest bandleaders of the century and revelled in live performance – he was known to insist upon going on stage even when quite ill and, towards the end of his life, refused to let his arthritis prevent him playing with the band, making his entrance in a motorized wheelchair. His extensive recording legacy provides a wealth of material for all to enjoy.

Basie's Basement
RCA Bluebird: ND 90630 (CD)

Compact Jazz: Count Basie
Verve: 831364-2 (CD)

Down For The Count
Jazz Up: JU 303 (CD)

Have A Nice Day
Verve: 824 867-2 (CD)

The Jubilee Alternatives
Hep Records: HEPCD 38 (CD)

The Original American Decca Recordings 1937–39
MCA: GRP 36112 (3 CDs, 3 cassettes)

Sidney Bechet (1897–1959)
(soprano sax, clarinet, tenor sax, bass sax, piano, bass, drums)

Sidney Bechet was born in St Antoine Street in New Orleans in 1897 and became famous as both a clarinettist and a saxophonist. From the remarkably young age of about nine he sat in and played alongside such illustrious bandleaders as Freddie Keppard. He started playing full-time in New Orleans bands at the still tender age of twelve and then moved on to Chicago, where he stayed for a couple of years working with Tony Jackson and again with his old friend Freddie Keppard. New York was his next stop, where he joined Will Marion Cook's Southern Syncopated Orchestra and toured Europe with them. Sidney Bechet had a unique sound on the clarinet and was the first jazz musician to attract serious attention from the classical world. The celebrated conductor Ernest Ansermet, one of the principal conductors of the Orchestre de la Suisse Romande, greatly admired Bechet's musicianship, for he had never heard anyone make such an extraordinarily engaging sound on the clarinet or the soprano saxophone.

Cook's band eventually broke up and Bechet joined Bennie Peyton's band in Paris, later moving back to New York where he was much in demand playing alongside many of the great blues singers like Mamie Smith and Rosetta Crawford under the direction of Clarence Williams. One of the high points in his career was working with Duke Ellington, who also loved his playing. However, always on the move, back and forth from the States to Europe, Bechet actually gave up serious playing for a short period to manage a tailor's shop in New York City, slotting in occasional gigs whenever he could. This followed a troubled time for Bechet – he was sent to prison in London over an incident involving a prostitute and was also concerned in a shooting incident in Paris, for which he spent time in a Paris jail. The move back to New York (but away from the jazz club scene) gave him the opportunity for a sedate lifestyle in tailoring. Bechet later formed a few small bands of his own and, after leading a band at Nick's (a jazz club in Greenwich Village), he did a number of concerts with Eddie Condon. He was firmly back in the jazz scene and loved every minute of it!

From the late Forties he spent most of his time in Paris, apart from a short spell in New York, when he made a number of very fine recordings. His playing was characterized by the use of heavy vibrato and his commitment to delivering forceful melodic lines in a sweeping demonstrative style. As much a character on as off the stage, he achieved national fame as a vaudeville figure and won numerous awards for his performances both live and on record. He had a number of students who also became famous in their own right including Johnny Hodges, Don Redman, Charlie Barnet, Woody Herman, John Coltrane and Bob Wilber, to name but a few; this gives some idea of what an influential player he was. He died of cancer on 14 May 1959; a statue has been erected in his memory in Antibes, where the town square is named after him. A truly outstanding musician and extraordinarily colourful character, Bechet was greatly missed on the jazz circuit.

RECOMMENDED LISTENING

Brussels World Fair Concert 1958
Vogue: 500203 (LP)

The Legendary Sidney Bechet
BMG/Bluebird: ND 86590 (CD)

Sidney Bechet, 1932-43: The Bluebird Sessions
BMG/Bluebird: ND 90317 (5 CDs)

Sidney Bechet and Friends
Verve: 840633-2 (CD)

Bix Beiderbecke (1903–31)
(cornet)

Leon Bix Beiderbecke was born in Davenport, Iowa into an upper middle-class family (who never forgave him for becoming a jazz musician) and developed an interest in music at an early age, playing both the piano and the cornet. By the time he was just sixteen he had begun to sit in with a number of local bands as a cornet player and at the age of nineteen he was enrolled at the Lake Forest Military Academy where he formed his first orchestra with Walter 'Cy' Wedge, a highly talented drummer. It seemed that he was so obsessive about music, that he never made the grade academically and was expelled in 1922, having failed to complete even the first year of study at the Academy.

Something of a wild man of jazz, Beiderbecke had a short career because of incessant problems with his health. He was a chronic alcoholic and, despite a great deal of compassion and help given by his friends, family and workmates, he died at the tragically young age of twenty-eight. Something of an enigmatic genius, Beiderbecke was consumed by a passion for music. He loved all kinds, especially classical, and was particularly fascinated by the music of Stravinsky, Debussy, Ravel and Delius, whose works embodied exotic scoring and colourful orchestrations.

During the last five years of his life he made a number of marvellous recordings which demonstrate his enormous talent. He worked a lot with the celebrated arranger Paul Whiteman, with whom much of his best work has been recorded and reissued, while other great collaborators include Jean Goldkette, Frankie Trumbauer and Hoagy Carmichael.

As a composer, Bix also experimented with writing music at the piano. His style was reminiscent of Debussy and Ravel and he gave titles to his pieces in a very similar vein to those of the French Impressionistic School – 'In a Mist', 'In the Dark' and 'Flashes' are early examples. One of the most talented and innovative of players, his death was a sad loss to music in general and the jazz world in particular. An exploration of his recorded works makes for much fascinating listening.

RECOMMENDED LISTENING

At The Jazz Band Ball, Volume 2
CBS 460825 (CD)

The Bix Beiderbecke Story
Deja Vu: DVRECD14 (CD)

Bix Lives!
Bluebird: ND 86845 (CD/LP/cassette)

Golden Age of Bix Beiderbecke
EMI: CDB 791 439-2 (CD)

Jazz Classics in Digital Stereo
BBC Records: BBC CD 601 (CD)

Acker Bilk (born 1929)
(clarinet)

Mention the clarinet in the context of trad jazz and, for many, particularly in the UK and Europe, the name of Acker Bilk will immediately spring to mind. He is responsible for creating a truly unique sound on the clarinet with a wide vibrato that he has featured in a variety of styles of music including trad and middle-of-the-road jazz.

Born Arthur Stanley Bilk in 1929, Acker was originally a blacksmith by trade, hailing from Somerset. He took up the clarinet in 1947 in order to pass the time while he was in the guardhouse in Egypt during the war. Like Chris Barber (see page 87), Acker Bilk joined the Ken Colyer Band and, after a relatively short time he, too, left to form his own band in Bristol, bringing it to London in 1957. It was named The Paramount Jazz Band and he has since performed all over the world with this unit in a variety of guises. His most famous tune is 'Stranger on the Shore', which he wrote as the theme tune for a children's television serial in the UK in the early Sixties. It's a tune that has caught the imagination of millions throughout the world and has become a most popular standard, selling over two million copies. Later, in 1976, Acker had another hit with a tune entitled 'Aria' that reached number five in the UK chart; the following year his highest chart-placed album, *Sheer Magic*, was released but is now unavailable.

Because of his wide appeal in the 'cross-over', middle-of-the-road market, he has not been taken as seriously as perhaps he might have been by true jazz aficionados. Though respected as a jazz clarinettist in many quarters, his image is now that of a proficient tunesmith and all-round entertainer, dressed in a bowler hat and a striped waistcoat, rather in the style of an Edwardian music hall artist.

RECOMMENDED LISTENING

Acker Bilk in Holland
Timeless: TTD 506/7 (CD/2LP)

At Sundown (with Humphrey Lyttelton)
Calligraph: CLG 027 (CD)

Blaze Away
Timeless: TTD 943/4 (CD/2LP)

Hits, Blues and Classics
Kaz: KAZCD 10 (CD)

That's My Home
Philips: 830778 (CD)

Art Blakey (1919–90)
(drums)

Best known for his band The Jazz Messengers, Art Blakey was born in Pittsburgh and was a talented bandleader and drummer who, through the channel of his own band, has played a major part in developing the talents of countless jazz musicians over the last thirty years, including Benny Golson, Freddie Hubbard, Wayne Shorter and Wynton Marsalis. Blakey became the leader of The Jazz Messengers in 1955, a band that was widely popular for some considerable time. He has made numerous records with other artists, such as Thelonious Monk (in 1957), Miles Davis, Fats Navarro and Buddy DeFranco. With his own band, the recorded catalogue is extensive – the first release was for Blue Note Records with the pianist Horace Silver.

His first ventures in music were entirely self-motivated – he taught himself to play the piano and formed his own big band at the age of fifteen. When a young pianist called Erroll Garner came along, Blakey moved from piano to drums, where he made an international reputation and career. Blakey always had an eye to the future trends in music and his style on the drums was undoubtedly one of the most influential of the bebop era, combining the best elements of bebop with gospel and blues-based music to form his own unique sound, incorporating polyrhythms and other African influences. Many drummers, in particular, picked up on this style of playing and incorporated it into their own – the early recordings of Weather Report bear many of these hallmarks and are well worth hearing, as is their later album *Heavy Weather*, which features a number of tracks in this vein. From the platform he provided for their talents, many of Blakey's most famous sidemen have gone on to have illustrious careers in their own right; perhaps the most notable is the trumpeter Wynton Marsalis who has achieved international fame and fortune by playing both jazz and classical music with equal talent and enthusiasm. Others whom Blakey helped on their way include Cedar Walton, Chick Corea and Keith Jarrett.

The Best of Art Blakey
EmArcy: 848245-2 (CD)

Buhaina's Delight
Blue Note: BNZ 295 (CD)

Indestructible!
Blue Note: B21Y-46429 (CD)

A Night At Birdland Volumes 1 and 2
Blue Note: CDP 746519 & 746520 (CD)

Ugetsu
Original Jazz Classics: OJC 090 (CD/LP/cassette)

Dave Brubeck (born 1920)
(piano)

Directly associated with one of the most famous jazz tunes of all time, 'Take Five', Dave Brubeck is undoubtedly among the best-known jazz artists to have emerged in the last fifty years. Christened David Warren, Brubeck came to prominence in the late Forties and early Fifties, touring the university campus scene and later the main venues in the United States. His rather heavy-handed piano playing and complex style of composing have been the subject of considerable controversy among musicians and critics, many of whom find his output a little too classically orientated to be classed as 'natural' swinging jazz. He had a formal musical upbringing – his family were all musicians – and he studied composition with the French composer Darius Milhaud and later with the innovative Arnold Schoenberg. Such a distinguished training explains why much of his creative output is very progressive harmonically and complicated in its structure – indeed, the same criticism is levelled at both his mentors. A serious musician in every sense, Brubeck wrote some enlightening statements at the time of his twenty-fifth anniversary reunion concert that help to explain his ideas on music and what it means to him. Part of his musical philosophy and ethos is to explore all music from African drum batteries to Bach, including Jelly Roll Morton, Stravinsky and Charlie Parker, among others, and one of his tasks and aims as a jazz improviser is to translate all emotions into a musical language which can deepen our understanding and awaken our senses.

He started making a succession of very successful records in 1949 for Coronet, which were later available on the Fantasy label. His quartet has toured the world's most prestigious jazz festivals and clubs to wide acclaim. His brother Howard broke new territory by writing a piece entitled 'Dialogue for Jazz Combo and Symphony' which was performed by the Dave Brubeck Quartet and the New York Philharmonic Orchestra conducted by Leonard Bernstein at the Carnegie Hall in 1959. This received mixed reviews, but Brubeck has gone on to delight audiences with his unique brand of jazz ever since. His quartet included the imaginative drummer Joe Morello and one of the most respected of alto saxophonists, Paul Desmond, who stayed in the band for some twenty-seven years and was replaced in 1978 by the great Gerry Mulligan and, shortly after his swift departure, by the innovative clarinettist Bill Smith.

RECOMMENDED LISTENING

25th Anniversary Reunion
A&M: 396998-2 (CD)

Blue Rondo
Concord Jazz: CCD 4317 (CD/cassette)

Interchanges '54
Sony Music: 4679172 (CD)

Quiet As The Moon
Limelight: 8208452 (CD)

Time Out
CBS Sony: 62068 (CD)

Benny Carter (born 1907)
(alto sax, trumpet, clarinet, vocals)

Benny Carter was born in New York in 1907 and is considered one of the most gifted and productive composer–arrangers in the entire history of jazz. He was also an exceptional saxophonist, specializing in the alto sax (although also playing clarinet, trumpet and occasionally trombone), and made a name for himself in the late Thirties as a bandleader of some distinction.

Unlike any other jazz 'great' mentioned in this book, he started out studying theology at Wilberforce University but quicky lost interest and became hooked on the idea of playing music. He joined a number of bands while in his early twenties, including those of Horace Henderson, Charlie Johnson (at Smalls), Fletcher Henderson, Chick Webb and, briefly, Duke Ellington. By 1933 he was sufficiently well known to launch his own big band and, in addition to doing intermittent work with this band, he toured Europe working on individual projects including concerts at Festivals, guesting in other people's bands and making a number of recordings. From 1936 he worked as the staff arranger for Henry Hall's BBC house radio band until in 1938 he returned to the United States via Scandinavia and France. He made some fine recordings while in France with the legendary jazz guitarist Django Reinhardt.

He re-formed his own band and continued to make a name as an arranger, working closely with Fletcher Henderson, Benny Goodman and others. As a performer he also formed a sextet with Dizzy Gillespie until in the mid-Forties he moved to California to write and arrange movie soundtracks in Hollywood. Among the most famous of these are *The Gene Krupa Story* and *Pennies From Heaven*; he can also be seen on camera in the films *The View From Pompey's Head* and *The Snows of Kilimanjaro*.

Carter has an exceptional all-round reputation. He is cited by many of the top saxophonists as a primary influence and, as an arranger, his work was the role model for many who followed him, particularly in the swing and big band fields. His arrangements bear many distinctive hallmarks, the most notable being his uncanny ability to make a small group or ensemble sound rich, beautiful and twice its actual size. Because of his affinity to the saxophone, his work involving the reed instruments is always beyond compare – try and find a copy of the now deleted album *Further Definitions* for some great examples, also his 'Symphony in Riffs' which is currently available as part of the *Living Era* series from ASV Records.

As recently as 1987, aged 80, he recorded the album *Central City Sketches* with his own band The American Jazz Orchestra and, while he is not internationally renowned among mainstream audiences, his work is proving immensely valuable to a whole generation of younger performers who thoroughly enjoy working with the great man in New York.

RECOMMENDED LISTENING

Central City Sketches
Music Masters: CIJD 60126X (CD)

The Chronological Benny Carter, 1940–41
Classics: CLASSICS 631 (CD)

Devil's Holiday (1933-34)
JSP: JSPCD 331 (CD)

In Paris 1935–1946
DRG:CDSW 8403 (CD)

Live and Well in Japan
JVC/Fantasy: VDJ 28010 (CD)

Ray Charles (born 1932) DIED 2004)
(vocals, piano)

Ray Charles was born Ray Charles Robinson in Georgia. He was blinded in an accident at the age of six and orphaned at thirteen. Despite these tragedies, he succeeded in making a great career as a musician – a fine songwriter, pianist, arranger and singer, Ray Charles is unquestionably one of the most influential artists in the whole history of jazz.

He moved to Seattle, Washington, in the early Fifties and through the medium of his own trio he developed a style incorporating an eclectic mixture of blues, gospel and jazz styles which laid the foundations of soul music as we know it today. His first big hit was the song 'What'd I Say?' which was released in 1959 and shot to number six in the US chart, being bought by a new audience made up of lovers of rock'n'roll, blues and gospel music. The song was later 'covered' by a number of other artists, including Jerry Lee Lewis, Bobby Darin and Elvis Presley, all of whom had much success with the track.

He went on to have a string of hits all around the world making constant live appearances to satisfy an eager public, always performing a beautifully balanced set of driving rhythmic numbers, gospel-based tracks and his famous hits like 'Georgia On My Mind' and 'Hit The Road, Jack'. In the late Fifties he worked with many of the all-time great names from the jazz world. He made an album with players from Count Basie and Duke Ellington bands, featuring arrangements by Ralph Burns and

Quincy Jones; its title became his nickname – 'The Genius'.

Ray Charles has won every award and accolade that there is to win and, as an astute businessman, he has made deals with record companies that only superstars like Michael Jackson, Prince and Bruce Springsteen have been able to make in recent years. He formed his own record company Tangerine in 1962 and through that outlet has released recordings of himself and a number of other artists, including Louis Jordan.

He continues to delight audiences all over the world and was recently in exceptionally fine form on Quincy Jones's most recent album *Back on the Block*, performing the song 'I'd Be Good For You' with such energy and vitality, you'd think he was in his twenties! Not immediately thought of as an out-and-out jazz singer, Ray Charles has nevertheless played an important role in the development of related genres and has worked alongside many of the great names of jazz – one of the finest entertainers of the twentieth century.

RECOMMENDED LISTENING

The Genius
Exel: XELCD 106 (CD)

Just Between Us
CBS Sony: 461183 2 (CD)

The Ray Charles Story
Deja Vu: DVRECD 02 (CD)

Ray Charles – Twenty Golden Greats
Deja Vu: DVCD 2005 (CD)

The Right Time
Atlantic: 241 119-2 (CD)

Kenny Clarke (1914–85)
(drums)

The drummer Kenny Clarke was among the most influential jazz musicians during the Forties and Fifties. He was born in Pittsburgh, Pennsylvania and is recognized as one of the greatest 'bop' drummers of all time playing alongside Miles Davis, Thelonious Monk, Tadd Dameron and Dizzy Gillespie, among others.

There was music in the Clarke household right from his earliest days – his father, a trombone player, introduced him to music, while his brothers played bass and drums respectively. Young Kenny started out as a professional musician in the Thirties with the Roy Eldridge Band but moved to New York in 1936 to join the Edgar Hayes Blue Rhythm Band with whom he toured for some years. Before the whole bebop movement started, he played with Benny Carter, Louis Armstrong, Ella Fitzgerald and Red Allen, later enjoying considerable success as leader of his own band.

Always seen as an innovator by his colleagues, he is widely acknowledged to be the founder of the modern jazz drumming technique that departed from the normal practice of using the bass drum as an essential rhythmic device in jazz beats. Clarke's style centred more on the incessant use of the ride cymbal to provide the very lifeblood of a track. He used the rest of the kit to punctuate solos, verses and choruses, often playing snap beats on the snare or bass drum to create interesting rhythmic devices within a rhythm pattern. His 'surprise' bass drum hits became known as 'bombs' and in later years Clarke was repeatedly asked by journalists about the significance of such a device. Kenny, by now completely fed up with such inane questions, came back with the response that he dropped these 'bombs' whenever his foot happened to get tired!

As a talented composer, Kenny 'Klook' Clarke also teamed up with Thelonious Monk to write the tune 'Epistrophy' and with Dizzy Gillespie to produce 'Salt Peanuts', both of which embody the rhythmic devices on which bebop cross-rhythms were based. He was one of the founder members of the prestigious Modern Jazz Quartet (replaced by Connie Kay when he left in 1956) and later went on to co-lead the Clarke-Boland Big Band with Francy Boland. He stayed with this band for ten years but in his later years concentrated more and more on recording, writing and teaching throughout Europe until his death near Paris in January 1985.

RECOMMENDED LISTENING

All Blues
MPS: MPS 68 227 (CD)

Bohemia After Dark
Denon: SV 0107 (CD)

Kenny Clarke Plays André Hodier
Polygram: 834542 (LP)

Live in Paris (1984)
EMI: 2M 256 64848 (cassette only)

Telefunken Blues
Denon: SV 0106 (CD)

Ornette Coleman (born 1930)
(alto sax, tenor sax, trumpet, violin)

Born in Fort Worth, Texas, in March 1930, Ornette Coleman is the man who in the late Fifties and early Sixties became known as the *enfant terrible* of the jazz world. He was one of the leaders of the avant-garde jazz movement and probably the most controversial.

His musical background is interesting. Largely self-taught, he picked up some musical training from his cousin, James Jordan, who was a music teacher, and although he started out playing the alto saxophone, he switched to the tenor some two years later at the age of sixteen. In his early years he was working regularly in R&B bands playing highly conventional music until he moved to Los Angeles in 1953, where he took a job as a lift operator, studying the theory of music in his spare time. His highly innovative ideas were quickly recognized and he was invited to make his first album, *Somethin' Else*, for Atlantic Records in 1958; it consisted of a batch of his own atonal compositions. As both performer and composer, Coleman met with widely varying critical responses, some praising his vision and originality, others, like Charlie Mingus, wondering if the composer could actually play the saxophone at all!

Coleman disregarded the conventions of traditional melody, rhythm and harmony, preferring a much freer approach to his music making. At the same time, contemporary classical music, in the hands of John Cage, Karlheinz Stockhausen and others, was moving in a similar direction – in fact, to many people's ears, what Coleman was doing was relatively mild by comparison. However, like many innovative, creative people Coleman had to stand by what he was doing in the face of some severe criticism from those around him. As a live performer he became quite belligerent in his commercial approach to concert performances and soon priced himself out of the established market – promoters simply were not prepared to pay Coleman the same fees that Brubeck could command when this man of avant-garde jazz had nothing like the same mass appeal or audience attraction.

So it was that Coleman would spend varying amounts of time out of the public eye, while he worked upon new material or concentrated on occasional recording projects. In 1972 he created a new piece entitled 'Skies of America' which was based on his own system of composition 'harmelody' in which the three elements of melody, harmony and rhythm were equal in importance. Rather than improvise on a tune or melody, Coleman found ways of improvising around the chord sequences themselves. 'Skies of America' was scored for a jazz quartet with the London Symphony Orchestra and received a rapturous response from all the musicians involved. The critics were not so enthusiastic and consequently CBS soon withdrew the recording; as a result the work is not widely known.

In the late Seventies he formed a group called Prime Time made up of a band of like-minded virtuoso electronic instrumentalists. The band performed and recorded quite extensively throughout the Seventies, under a record label called Caravan of Dreams. The first two albums, again caused some controversy – *Opening the Caravan of Dreams* and *Prime Design/Time Design* were later followed by a double album entitled *In All Languages*. These are all well worth listening to if avant-garde jazz captures your interest. In 1986 Coleman joined forces with the guitarist Pat Metheny to produce an interesting album in *Song X* which also features Charlie Haden, Coleman's son Denardo (on drums) and Jack DeJohnette.

Ornette Coleman is one of the greatest talents of the last thirty years or so. His most recent offerings through the band Prime Time are a fascinating mix of avant-garde jazz with elements of rock and funk and are currently reaching a wide audience.

RECOMMENDED LISTENING

Dancing In Your Head
A&M: CDA 0807 (CD)

In All Languages
Caravan of Dreams: DREAM 009 (CD)

Live in Milano, 1968
Jazz Up: JU 310 (CD)

Song X
Geffen: 9240962 (CD)

Tomorrow Is The Question
Original Jazz Classics: OJC 342 (CD/LP/cassette)

John Coltrane (1926–67)
(tenor sax, alto sax, soprano sax, flute)

John Coltrane was born in Hamlet, North Carolina into a musical family – his father was an amateur musician and a tailor by trade, but was sufficiently interested in music to start John on the saxophone and clarinet while he was at school. Needless to say, Coltrane's talent emerged early and he was soon playing in bands and showing an extraordinary degree of talent. He studied music formally at Granoff Studios and later at the Ornstein School of Music in Philadelphia, making his professional debut at the age of nineteen in a cocktail combo band. From there his first serious jazz job was playing in Joe Webb's Rhythm and Blues band with the descriptively named singer 'Big Maybelle'.

The next seven or eight years saw him playing in a variety of well-known bands – with Eddie 'Cleanhead' Vinson (1947–48), Dizzy Gillespie (1949–51), Earl Bostic (1952–53) and Johnny Hodges (1953–54). However, his big break came when Miles Davis heard him playing and asked him to join his band in 1955. This quintet was achieving widespread popularity in the jazz world and Coltrane made a huge hit, especially with the solo that he played on the recording of *Round About Midnight*. The stark contrast between the cool-sounding Miles Davis and the extremely hard-hitting tenor saxophone sound of John Coltrane made for some very exciting arrangements and this band became the one that most other jazzmen were keeping their eyes and ears on.

From 1957 to 1959 Coltrane worked with Thelonious Monk, Red Garland and Donald Byrd. It was a critical period for his development and he was constantly on a voyage of discovery and experimentation, the results of which had an enormous effect on the whole jazz movement. With Thelonious Monk (who was also innovative and inventive), Coltrane was able to move away from the conventional reliance on the basic chord structures of a piece to dictate what could be played; instead he developed a way of improvising around the notes of all the different related scales to each chord, often at break-neck speed. He is quoted as saying that when he was working with Monk they were lucky to get things together because each would mentally be following a completely different set of chords to a tune – 'everybody tried anything they wanted to . . .' Naturally, to many people's ears, the results sounded quite foreign and beyond all comprehension, but to those who were involved in jazz and appreciated the finer points of harmonic development, key relationships and the art of improvisation, the results were staggering and a source of great inspiration.

The subject of much discussion and criticism, Coltrane's blistering style of improvising was given the description of 'sheets of sound' – the essence of which is that he delivered cascades of notes based on so many different modes and scales in a very short time span, that the results blew past you. The critic John S. Wilson once said that 'he often plays his tenor sax as if he were determined to blow it apart, but his desperate attacks almost invariably lead nowhere.' On the other hand, he was hailed by others as being beyond compare, a true innovator and 'the most individual young tenor player'. My favourite quote about Coltrane is that by Zita Carno, who wrote in Jazz Review 'The only thing you can, and should, expect from John Coltrane is the unexpected.'

He had terrible problems with drugs and alcohol and lived life to the absolute extreme. This also applied to his perception of music – he was constantly exploring new idioms and incorporating new styles into his playing. He became increasingly interested in Arabic, Eastern and Asian music, drawing from each their different scale patterns and key structures and fusing them into a new kind of music. He signed a deal with Atlantic Records in 1960 and from this period there was a move away from the 'sheets of sound' to a more lyrical, melodic approach to his music. He took great inspiration from a very simple melody by the celebrated composer of musicals, Richard Rodgers, in the tune 'My Favorite Things'. He performed this piece on countless occasions and a number of recordings remain in the catalogues to this day. He played the tune on the somewhat nasal-sounding soprano saxophone and his improvisations generally took their inspiration from the repetitive, monotonous elements of Indian and Asian music.

Through the early and middle Sixties he continued to explore the music of many nations and produced albums like *Olé Coltrane*, *Africa/Brass* and *India*, all of which make fascinating listening. He also became deeply interested in religion and this had an intense, direct effect on his music perhaps best shown in *A Love Supreme*. Coltrane wrote the lyrics himself, following his spiritual awakening in the late Fifties, and they are a very personal testament to his religious convictions, containing cries for help and expressions of confusion, unworthiness, and guilt over his drug addiction. His alcohol and drug dependencies caused Coltrane many problems and this serious inner conflict is clearly demonstrated in his music.

By 1965 Coltrane was firmly established as part of the New York avant-garde jazz fraternity. His music was, indeed, totally free in every sense – melodically, harmonically and rhythmically. On 28 June 1965 he recorded an album of considerable historic importance entitled *Ascension*. It featured all the great avant-garde jazzmen of the day, including Pharaoh Sanders and Archie Shepp (tenor saxes), Freddie Hubbard and Dewey Johnson (trumpets), John Tchicai and Marion Brown (alto saxes), Art Davis and Jimmy Garrison (basses), McCoy Tyner on piano and Elvin Jones on drums – a staggering line-up, if ever there was one for this kind of project. The result was quite shocking for some. Marion Brown even remarked that you could use the record to heat up an apartment on a cold winter's day! It was, however, Coltrane's perception of the transcendence of man to God – an ascension into heaven. It was a deeply personal, spiritual and musical statement.

Towards the end of his life, he played in a band that featured his wife, Alice, who was a pianist, organist, harpist and composer. They were extremely close and Alice has since gone on to develop the elements of Coltrane's latter-day styles from where her husband left off. Alice's religious convictions, like John's, play an important part in her creative output, most notably in the album which she issued in 1970, featuring tracks by John with string overdubs of her own. In another album, *Lord of Lords*, she has re-orchestrated a piece by Stravinsky following a 'divine visitation' from the late composer who, she claims, has given her strict instructions as to the orchestration of the work.

John Coltrane died tragically in 1967, totally exhausted by his own intensity of being. He did everything to excess, physically and mentally draining himself of life force. He will be remembered as one of the most influential jazz musicians of the last fifty years and as the man who created total freedom in music – opening up new grounds for harmony, rhythm and melody, and extending the boundaries of improvisation.

RECOMMENDED LISTENING

Africa/Brass Volumes 1 and 2
MCA: MCAD 42001 (CD)

Blue Train
Blue Note: CDP 7460952 (CD/cassette)

Giant Steps
Atlantic: 781337-2 (CD/cassette)

John Coltrane Collection
Deja Vu: DVCD 2037 (CD)

Meditations
MCA: MCAD 39139 (CD)

My Favorite Things
Atlantic: 782346-2 (CD)

Ken Colyer (1928–88)
(cornet, trumpet, guitar, vocals)

Ken Colyer was a self-taught trumpet player, who was born in East Anglia in the UK in 1928. He took up music while in the merchant navy and formed his first band, the Crane River Jazz Band, in 1949 after the war. In 1953, having rejoined the merchant navy, Colyer jumped ship at New Orleans and started playing with local bands. He was imprisoned for overstaying his allotted time in the States and came back to the UK as something of a folk hero.

He was one of the most influential figures in the British jazz scene and played a leading part in the advent of the style known as 'skiffle'. He played on numerous albums during the mid-Fifties, developing a unique 'band sound' and demonstrating what a very perceptive all-round musician he was. He had clear views on music and how one should listen to music and often said that his band would make only one excellent performance of a piece in every six – sometimes, he claimed, the odds might even be longer. His point was that music should not be taken too flippantly and that it always deserved complete attention from the artist as well as from the listener.

In the late Sixties Colyer became very ill and underwent a course of radiotherapy to control his stomach cancer. This, understandably, took its toll on his artistry but after a few years he made some further very worthwhile contributions to an extensive recorded legacy. He sang on a number of tracks and while his music sounds, to many, somewhat restrained, it inspired a whole generation of blues and rock bands who were up and coming in the early Sixties. Many of the best British jazzmen have worked alongside Ken Colyer; they include Chris Barber, Alexis Korner, Acker Bilk and Monty Sunshine.

Colyer's health failed again in the mid-Eighties, when he stopped playing altogether and went to live in a caravan in the south of France.

RECOMMENDED LISTENING

Live 1953–54
Limelight: 8208792 (CD)

Painting The Clouds With Sunshine
Black Lion: BLC 760501 (CD)

Ragtime Revisited
Joy: JOY-CD-2 (CD)

Spirituals Volume 1
Joy: JOY-CD-5 (CD)

Too Busy
CMJ: CMJ 008 (CD)

Eddie Condon (1905-73)
(guitar)

Hailing from Goodland, Indiana and christened Albert Edwin Condon, Eddie Condon carved a unique position for himself in the jazz world as both performer and promoter. He was raised in Momence and Chicago Heights where he taught himself to play the ukulele and later the guitar. He showed enormous early promise and by the age of fifteen or sixteen was regularly playing in bands with a team of very talented white musicians who went on to develop what became known as the 'Chicago Sound' of the twenties, closely imitating the sounds of their black heroes.

In 1928 he moved to New York City where he performed extensively and started promoting jazz gigs and jam sessions. His first recordings were made for the first independent jazz record label, Commodore. By the mid-Forties, his now famous jam sessions had established quite a following and soon a series of concerts was booked in the Town Hall. He also opened up a nightclub of his own in Greenwich Village and in 1948 began his pioneering TV series which brought new recognition and a wider audience to Dixieland jazz.

Condon was a keen writer and wrote many excellent books, including his autobiography, *We Call It Jazz*, which contains many humorous and enlightening stories of the great jazz legends and is well worth reading. He was very much a social animal and as happy to be talking and drinking with his audiences as to be performing. There are many stories about how laid back he was about his playing; it is true that one often has to listen very hard to his recordings to hear the sounds of his guitar as he was extremely economical and minimalist in what he played, both in terms of the number of notes and the volume at which he performed. Nevertheless, he proved to be an influential player and a fine all-round talent who made a significant contribution to the jazz movement.

RECOMMENDED LISTENING

The Definitive Eddie Condon And His Jazz Concert All Stars: Volume 1
Stash: ST-CD-530 (CD)

Eddie Condon Floor Show: Jazz on the Air
Jazzline: JL 20803 (CD)

Eddie Condon Live in 1944
Jass: JCD 634 (CD)

Eddie Condon Volume 1 (1938)
Commodore Classics: 824 054 (CD)

Town Hall Concerts Volume 6
Jazzology Records: JCECD 1011/12 (CD)

Chick Corea (born 1941)
(piano, keyboards)

Born Armando Anthony Corea in 1941, 'Chick' (as he later became known) has developed a reputation as one of the finest all-round jazz keyboardists of the last twenty-five years, alongside Keith Jarrett and Herbie Hancock. His first interest in jazz was aroused by the recordings of Charlie Parker and Bud Powell, which were frequently played on the gramophone by his father, who was an active musician in the dance band scene.

Chick was sent to the Juilliard School of Music where he took advanced piano lessons – his musical ability gave him a wide repertoire incorporating both classical and jazz. But it was jazz to which he turned for a career when he was invited to replace the vibraphonist Gary Burton in Stan Getz's quartet. Throughout the Sixties, Chick Corea was recruited as a sideman performing with a number of well-known jazz musicians such as Herbie Mann, Hubert Laws, Blue Mitchell and Mongo Santamaria. In 1968 he was asked to replace Herbie Hancock in the Miles Davis band to record the now classic albums *In A Silent Way* and *Bitches Brew*, on which he played acoustic and electric pianos.

Shortly after this period with Miles Davis he formed his own group, Circle, with bassist Dave Holland (who had also been in the Davis band) and Barry Altschul. They played well together but, forever in search of new creative and artistic challenges, Corea then formed another band called Return To Forever with the virtuoso Latin percussionist Airto Moreira and singer Flora Purim. Stanley Clarke was the bassist and the guitarist Al DiMeola was also featured from time to time. Return To Forever was extremely successful, producing six albums, three of which made the top forty in the Billboard pop chart in the Seventies.

Possessing limitless flexibility and an ability to perform

adeptly in all styles of music, Chick Corea is equally at home on either the piano or electronic keyboards, playing bebop, Latin, free jazz or classical. He has recorded the *Concerto for Two Pianos* by Mozart and also written a series of *Piano Improvisations* and *Children's Songs* in the classical genre. In recent years, as well as giving innumerable concerts as a solo pianist, he has appeared in concert with the aforementioned vibraphonist Gary Burton, as an accompanist to his singer wife, Gayle Moran, and with his trio The Elektric Band, alongside bassist John Patitucci and drummer Dave Weckl.

RECOMMENDED LISTENING

Compact Jazz: Chick Corea
Polydor: 831365-2 (CD)

The Elektric Band
GRP: GRPD 9535 (CD)

Now He Sings, Now He Sobs
Blue Note: CDP 790 055 (CD)

Piano Improvisations Volumes 1 and 2
ECM: 1014/1020 (CD/LP)

Return To Forever
ECM: 8119782 (CD)

John Dankworth (born 1927)
(alto sax, clarinet)

John Philip William Dankworth stands at the very pinnacle of the British jazz scene, having achieved mass popularity through television and radio exposure in a partnership with his jazz vocalist wife, Cleo Laine. John received a formal musical training at the Royal Academy of Music where he studied the clarinet, composition and arranging.

From the early Forties his interest in trad jazz led him towards playing in bands but when he discovered bebop he decided to work on the transatlantic liners in order to make his way to New York where he could enjoy the music live. This had a profound influence on Dankworth and fuelled his imagination both as a performer and as a composer.

He has since made a highly successful career both as a player and as a composer/arranger. His early jobs in bands included working with the Tito Burns Sextet (where he played alongside the celebrated Ronnie Scott on tenor saxophone) and as a founder member of Club 11. In 1950 he decided to form his own band, the Johnny Dankworth Seven, which featured Cleo Laine, whom he married in 1958. Since that time, Dankworth has kept the band going on a regular basis and has also acted as musical director for Cleo Laine.

As an arranger he has been extremely active, his first efforts being taken up by the Ted Heath band. More recently his activities in this field have focused on music for television and films, with occasional cross-over pieces written in a classical/jazz genre, such as an entertaining short piece for the clarinettist Emma Johnson, 'Song for Emma', and the more extensive 'Fair Oak Fusions' written for the 'cellist Julian Lloyd-Webber.

Still active as a performer, John Dankworth plays regularly at the festival at the family home in Wavendon, bringing together a wonderful collection of players for these occasions. In his own band he features the extra-ordinarily gifted pianist John Horler (who is also well known for his work in the London circuit with players like Tony Coe) and his son Alec, an exceptional bass guitarist.

RECOMMENDED LISTENING

Innovations
Pickwick: PWK 059 (CD)

The Roulette Years
Roulette: CDROU 1034 (CD)

Symphonic Fusions
Pickwick: PCD 842 (CD)

The Vintage Years 1953–1959
Sepia: RSCD2014; RSK2014 (CD/cassette)

Miles Davis (1926–91)
(trumpet, flugelhorn)

Miles Dewey Davis was born into an affluent family in Alton, Illinois in 1926 and was brought up in St Louis. His father was a landowner and a dentist by trade, so Miles escaped the deprived childhood that was the lot of many great jazz performers. He was given a trumpet for his thirteenth birthday and immediately showed great promise and enthusiasm. While he was learning, he went to listen to, and meet, people like Charlie Parker, Dizzy Gillespie and Clark Terry, all of whom had a profound influence on the young trumpeter. When he was just sixteen years old, Sonny Stitt heard him play and said, 'You look like a man named Charlie Parker and you play like him, too. Come with us!' It's ironic that his mother wouldn't let him accept because he would miss his last year at school. However, when he was sent off to study at the Juilliard School of Music just a year later, he quickly found his niche in the small 52nd Street clubs in New York, playing alongside these very same musicians. He also played with Coleman Hawkins, Billy Eckstine and as part of the Benny Carter Band – all in all, quite an auspicious start to his career and the foundation of his later reputation as one of the world's most distinguished jazz trumpeters.

Between 1946 and 1948 he made a number of now classic recordings with Charlie Parker and in September 1948 he led his own group at New York's Royal Roost Club where the works of Gerry Mulligan, John Lewis and Gil Evans were performed. Some claim this to be the real birth of bebop, while real jazz purists feel the style was set later by the 1955 quintet featuring Davis with John Coltrane, Red Garland, Paul Chambers and Philly 'Joe' Jones. The early Fifties saw a long period of inactivity through his dependency on heroin and Miles was only really in good shape for public performances again in 1954, after which he made a very big impact on the jazz world with the quintet.

In 1957, Davis made history yet again, following his work in the big band scene with Gil Evans, who created a whole set of arrangements featuring the inimitable sound of Davis's trumpet set against the subtle and extraordinary sound of his band. Just one year later, the album *Kind of Blue* was released – an album featuring Miles's small jazz-combo band which proved, at that time, to be the epitome of avant-garde expression. Its influence was immeasurable. Based on modal themes and jazz scale patterns, it caused many serious jazz musicians to change direction thereafter, including two famous members of the band in Julian 'Cannonball' Adderley and John Coltrane.

In the Sixties Miles changed style again and again. He was seen as one of the main gurus to have emerged from the 'Cool' period of jazz. He was instrumental in developing the talents of people like the keyboardist Herbie Hancock, saxophonist Wayne Shorter, pianist Chick Corea, drummer Tony Williams and the celebrated acoustic bass player Ron Carter. The reunion with Gil Evans produced a host of classic tracks featuring a large-scale band in which Evans had left out the traditional saxophone section and replaced it with an unusual combination of instruments, including the french horn, flute, clarinet, bass clarinet, alto saxophone and tuba. Miles was also featured playing the flugelhorn on a number of tracks – its mellower and darker sound enabling him to deliver some distinctively haunting and moody solos.

By the early part of the Seventies Miles was no longer considered part of the mainstream jazz fraternity, preferring to spend time working on rock music projects. In 1975, after a serious car accident, extensive problems with drug taking, and a shooting incident which led to his arrest, it seemed that we had seen the last of Miles Davis on the concert platform or in a recording studio. Six years later, however, *The Man With The Horn* was released to great critical reviews and he set off on another journey of musical development.

Miles Davis was a musician who was always open to new influences and trends in the contemporary music scene. He much admired the work of the guitarist Jimi Hendrix and was able to incorporate some of his stylistic traits and devices into his own unique power of expression, while Hendrix himself openly acknowledged the influence that Miles had on his own playing. A prime example of his later moves away from the standard jazz or jazz rock scene is the album *Tutu* on which Marcus Miller was the important collaborator. It is a dynamic album that set the benchmark for others.

Davis was once asked whether he preferred composing or playing and answered with the enigmatic 'I can't answer that. There's a certain feeling you get from playing, but never from writing – and when you're playing it's like composing anyway . . .' A remarkable man who, despite his drug addiction and alcohol abuse, has emerged as one of the true musical geniuses of the last hundred years.

Recommended Listening

Birth of the Cool
Capitol: CDP 792862 (CD)

Compact Jazz: Miles Davis
Verve: 838 254 (CD)

Kind of Blue
CBS: 32109 (CD/cassette)

Miles Ahead
CBS: 460606 (CD/cassette)

Miles Davis: The Columbia Years 1955–85
Columbia: 4632462 (CD)

Milestones
CBS: 460827 (CD/cassette)

Siesta
Warner Brothers 925 655-2 (CD/LP/cassette)

Tutu
Warner Brothers 925 490 (CD/LP/cassette)

Johnny Dodds (1892–1940)
(clarinet, alto sax)
and Warren 'Baby' Dodds
(1898–1959) (drums)

For a New Orleans jazzman, Johnny Dodds has the unique distinction of having been taught to play the clarinet by a classical clarinettist. This did not seem to affect his natural affinity to jazz and he had his first break with Kid Ory's Band in 1911, at the age of nineteen. Like many of his contemporaries, he moved to Chicago where he played with a variety of bands, including those of King Oliver and Freddie Keppard. He took over as leader of the Freddie Keppard Band in 1924 and remained in the job at Bert Kelly's Stables for some six years. He was a brilliant musician and in demand for almost everyone's records; some of his best work in the recording studio was with Louis Armstrong's Hot Five and Hot Seven. Unlike the stereotype jazzman, Dodds was a sober, drug-free individual who played consistently well throughout his entire career, unharmed by the alcohol and illegal substances which played havoc with many of his colleagues.

Curiously, he and his brother (Warren 'Baby' Dodds) fell on hard times during the early Thirties and Johnny ended up driving taxis for a living, playing for fun in his spare time. He went to New York on only one occasion and that was in 1938 to take part in a recording session for Decca. A severe heart attack the following year put paid to any further work in the jazz clubs and he died just one year later, having earned a fine reputation as one of the best clarinettists from New Orleans.

★   ★   ★

The younger brother of clarinettist Johnny Dodds, Warren 'Baby' Dodds's career followed much the same pattern as that of his brother. They performed together in Freddie Keppard's Band, Warren, a drummer, having previously performed extensively on the Chicago circuit. He made numerous recordings with a variety of artists but was often under fire from the established jazz critics, some of whom found his playing unnecessarily flamboyant and undisciplined. Louis Armstrong, however, was a great admirer of his playing, as was the clarinettist and saxophonist, Sidney Bechet.

He suffered a stroke in the late Forties and another in 1952, after which time his health declined so severely that partial paralysis set in and he was forced to quit altogether. Despite the comments of the critics, 'Baby' Dodds was widely regarded as one of the greatest true New Orleans jazz drummers ever.

RECOMMENDED LISTENING

Blue Clarinet Stomp
Bluebird: ND 82293 (CD/LP)

Jazz Classics in Digital Stereo: Volume 9 (1923-29)
BBC: BBCCD 603 (CD)

Johnny Dodds 1926-1940
Affinity: AFS 1023 (3CDs)

Johnny Dodds Volume 2
Village Jazz: VILCD 0172 (CD)

Jimmy Dorsey (1904–57)
(alto sax, baritone sax, clarinet, trumpet)

Jimmy Dorsey was born into a musical family in Shenan-doah, Pennsylvania and was the elder brother of the trombonist, Tommy Dorsey (*see* below). Their father led a local brass band in which Jimmy made his debut at the age of eight. He played in a number of local bands, including his own Dorsey's Novelty Six and Dorsey's Wild Canaries, and then joined the Scranton Sirens as saxophonist. A marvellous alto player, he was eventually spotted by Ed Kirkeby and joined his group The California Ramblers in 1924. Jimmy did a lot of recording work at this time and toured with Paul Whiteman, Red Nichols and Jean Goldkette. In the early Thirties the Dorsey brothers formed their own successful big band but they split up in 1935. They both appeared in the movie *The Fabulous Dorseys*.

Because he moved to the world of the big band and commercial dance band music, Jimmy Dorsey is not highly thought of by the jazz purists but he was never-theless a fine exponent of his art. Herb Stanford wrote an excellent biography of the two brothers, *The Dorsey Years*.

Jimmy Dorsey at the 400 Restaurant 1946
Hep Records: HEPCD 41 (CD)

Pennies From Heaven
ASV: AJA 5052 (CD)

Perfida
Laserlight: 15768 (CD)

Tommy Dorsey (1905–56)
(trombone, trumpet)

Tommy Dorsey's career follows very closely that of his elder brother Jimmy, the sax player. He too was born in Shenandoah and played in the family bands but had a longer and closer association with Paul Whiteman than Jimmy did. Tommy was a superb musician, renowned for the beautiful tone quality of his trombone playing and his extraordinary virtuoso technique. One of his most famous tracks is the ballad 'I'm Getting Sentimental Over You', which he first recorded in September 1932 – this track demonstrates his wonderfully smooth, round sound and has become something of a trade mark for him.

Following the formation of his own band in the mid-Thirties, when the two brothers parted company, Tommy worked with many of the great jazz musicians as well as with some of the great singers such as Frank Sinatra and Connie Haynes. He appeared in several films, including the musicals *The Fleet's In* and *Shall We Dance?* as well as the biographical *The Fabulous Dorseys*. The brothers got back together in 1953 and formed a new band, mainly led by Tommy. So successful was this new band that they went on to have their own television programme, *Stage Show*, for CBS.

A highly talented musician, Tommy Dorsey was perhaps most at home playing what may best be termed popular music, not 'real' jazz. His biggest hit was with the track 'Boogie-Woogie', which sold over four million copies; other hits include 'Sunny Side of the Street' and 'Song of India'. He died suddenly at his country home after choking on some food – a tragic end to a great career.

RECOMMENDED LISTENING

The All Time Hit Parade Rehearsals
Hep Records: HEP 39 (CD)

Stardust (with Frank Sinatra)
Bluebird: ND 90627 (CD)

Yes Indeed!
Bluebird: ND 904499 (CD/LP/cassette)

Duke Ellington (1899–1974)
(piano)

Born in Washington, DC in 1899, Edward Kennedy 'Duke' Ellington is certainly one of the most famous names in big band music. He was a fine pianist and had a truly extraordinary talent as an arranger and composer. Offered a scholarship to study at the prestigious Pratt Institute in Brooklyn, New York, Ellington turned it down in favour of becoming a pianist. His earliest work was as a semi-professional musician providing bands for parties and dances and he added to his earnings by painting signs and posters. By the time that he married Edna Thompson in 1918, he was enjoying considerable success as a bandleader in and around Washington, but he had a rough few months when his first attempts to work in New York failed. Times were hard and it was difficult to break in on a new scene and the great Duke Ellington felt pretty despondent.

However, in 1923, with his band The Washingtonians, Ellington made a big impact at the Kentucky Club in downtown New York, where he had been persuaded to return by the pianist Fats Waller. It was during a residency at this club that Ellington developed his early arrangements and his musical style as we know it today. Ellington's arrangements are unique because of his gift for creating new sounds and textures for the instruments at his disposal and also because of the solo contributions made by the principal players in his band. He made it his business to surround himself with a fascinating mixture of the finest talents around: these included Bubber Miley (trumpet), Joe Nanton (trombone), Harry Carney (saxophones), Fred Guy (banjo), Sonny Greer (drums), Wellman Braud (bass) and, of course, the 'Duke' himself on piano.

The arrangements that made Ellington's band sound unique came into being by a rather curious process. Individual players would contribute various elements and all these ideas would be used to construct the finished product – always overseen and directed by Ellington himself. Most commonly, Ellington, Billy Strayhorn or one of the band members would suggest a tune and during the ensuing rehearsal session Ellington would listen intently to the contributions, select the best of all the ideas and weave them into the distinctive 'Ellington sound'. He was a master of orchestration and had a great gift for knowing what worked well for all types of tunes. He is perhaps most famous for his own compositions like 'Satin Doll', 'Sophisticated Lady', 'It Don't Mean a Thing If It Ain't Got That Swing', 'Mood Indigo' and 'Solitude', all of which demonstrate his wide-ranging talent.

Throughout the Thirties and Forties, Ellington broke so much new ground in the big band field that almost everyone since has been influenced by his work in one way or another. With the tune 'Caravan', recorded in 1937, on which he collaborated with the trombonist Juan Tizol, he led the official 'mainstream' way towards Latin Jazz. Tizol was from Puerto Rico and inspired Ellington to incorporate Latin American rhythms, which, in turn, paved the way for the Cuban Jazz movement that is so popular at jazz clubs and festivals today. All the members of Ellington's band made a significant musical contribution – there were no 'passengers'. The band changed personnel several times as was to be expected throughout such a long and varied career; among the superstars who played with him on a regular basis were artists like Johnny Hodges, Ben Webster, Harry Carney, Barney Kessel and Lawrence Brown. Ellington harnessed their talents to produce some of the finest popular music of this century.

Black, Brown and Beige
RCA Bluebird: 86641 (3CDs/4 cassettes)

The Blanton-Webster Years
Bluebird: 85659 (3CDs/4 cassettes)

The Complete Duke Ellington Volumes 1-5
CBS: 462985/6/7/8/9 (CDs/cassettes)

Duke Ellington 1929
Classics: 569 (CD)

Duke Ellington and Friends
Verve: 833 291-2 (CD)

Money Jungle
Blue Note: B21Y 46398 (CD/LP/cassettes)

Solos, Duets and Trios
Bluebird: ND 82178 (CD)

Bill Evans (1929–80)
(piano)

The pianist Bill Evans stands as one of the most innovative
and highly respected pianists to emerge in the last thirty
years. He changed the perception of the piano within
the jazz medium by his completely new approach to the
instrument's capabilities. Perhaps the most interesting
device he developed was that of the voicing of harmonies
between the two hands, with almost rippling arpeggiated

figures in the right hand, and the left concentrating on providing rhythmic punctuations and counter-melody lines that colour the harmonic textures.

He was a deeply private, introspective individual whose main interests in music were centred around the standard classic tunes of the jazz repertoire. A brilliant composer as well as a virtuoso pianist, his own compositions feature on a number of albums including *Interplay* and *Conversations With Myself* (*see* below).

A frequent performer with people like Miles Davis and Julian 'Cannonball' Adderley, Bill Evans gained the respect of every musician that came into contact with him. Miles Davis once commented 'I sure learned a lot from Bill Evans. He plays the piano the way it should be played.' Evans also formed his own trio with bass player Scott LaFaro and drummer Paul Motian (who can be heard on the CD *Get Into Jazz*). This combo had enormous success both live and on records and their particularly auspicious engagement at the Village Vanguard in New York in June 1961 resulted in a superb album currently available on CD. LaFaro died tragically in a car accident just ten days after this performance and Evans withdrew into a period of severe depression which lasted well over a year. The bass player Chuck Israels managed to persuade Bill Evans to come back to work and the results he produced from this time on rank among his finest. He won five Grammy Awards for his album *Conversations With Myself*; in this he used multi-track recording to improvise over a previously recorded improvisation – a technique that was way ahead of its time.

Evans went on to play in a number of small groups featuring Eddie Gomez, Marty Morell and sometimes

Eliot Zigmund, and took his previously successful recording project one step further by releasing *New Conversations* in 1973; it is one of his finest achievements. Like many others around him, he was dependent on drugs and alcohol and died from a bleeding ulcer in a New York hospital in September 1980.

RECOMMENDED LISTENING

At The Montreux Jazz Festival
Verve: 827844-2 (CD)

Compact Walkman Jazz: Bill Evans
Verve: 831366-2 (CD)

Conversations With Myself
Verve: 8219884-2 (CD)

Explorations
Original Jazz Classics: OJC 037 (CD/LP/cassette)

New Jazz Conceptions
Original Jazz Classics: OJC 035-2 (CD/LP/cassette)

Sunday At The Village Vanguard
Original Jazz Classics: OJC 140 (CD/LP/cassette)

Gil Evans (1912–88)
(piano, arranger, composer)

Gil Evans was born in Toronto, Canada, of Australian parentage and brought up in British Columbia and

California. He was a self-taught musician who played the piano but was really more at home as an arranger and a composer.

Following the Second World War, Evans re-joined the Claude Thornhill Band and experimented with the most unusual style of arrangements the jazz world had ever encountered. The results were magnificent, bringing to jazz elements of French Impressionistic music from the classical genre and introducing instruments like the French horn and the tuba – quite a departure from the normal big band line-up. His work caught the attention of many of the jazz leaders and his later associations, with Miles Davis in particular, gave rise to much of the finest jazz of the late Fifties and Sixties.

His work is best known through the collaborations with Miles – he was a key contributor to the classic album *The Birth of the Cool*, for which he actually wrote two of the best tracks in 'Boplicity' and 'Moon Dreams'. Some years later the partnership was renewed and the two worked together on *Miles Ahead, Porgy and Bess, Sketches of Spain, At Carnegie Hall* and *Quiet Nights*.

Evans occasionally worked under his own name as an artist; his most popular album is *Out of the Cool*, on which he brought together the soprano and alto saxophonists Steve Lacy, Julian 'Cannonball' Adderley and Lee Konitz. The album is without doubt a masterpiece and has had a profound influence on arrangers. Having previously broken totally new ground with his instinctive approach to the use of orchestral instruments within the jazz field, Evans produced an all-electric album, *Svengali*, in 1973 which featured a very young David Sanborn on alto sax. This was a true jazz rock project that was funky, free and powerful. It has been described as a unique blend of the music of Charlie Parker with that of Jimi Hendrix and it's interesting to note that Evans was invited to work with Hendrix the following year. He recorded several compositions of Hendrix over the next twelve months and followed a punishing schedule of engagements, recordings and TV work until his death in 1988. One of his last commissions was to arrange the Jimi Hendrix tune 'Little Wing' for Sting's album *Nothing Like The Sun*.

Evans was a source of great inspiration to everyone with whom he worked – Miles Davis is the obvious example, but in a wider context, his brilliant work in the field of orchestration has been particularly influential to writers of jazz, classical and film music.

RECOMMENDED LISTENING

Gil Evans Plays The Music of Jimi Hendrix
Bluebird: ND 84809 (CD)

Into The Hot
Impulse: MCAD 39104 (CD)

Live At Sweet Basil
Electric Bird: K23P 6355/6 (CD/LP)

Out Of The Cool
MCA: MCACD 9653 (CD)

Paris Blues
Owl: 049 (CD/LP)

Ella Fitzgerald (born 1918)
(vocals)

Born in Newport News, Virginia, Ella Fitzgerald was discovered while singing in an amateur show at the Harlem Opera House at the tender age of sixteen. Winning first prize, she was immediately invited to join the band led by the drummer Chick Webb, which she later led when Webb died. Engagements followed in all manner of venues, from nightclubs to theatres, jazz clubs and concert halls. It was already quite clear that Ella Fitzgerald was on the road to stardom as a singer of the most consummate talent. Her voice has a clarity and warmth of tone that is as engaging in a ballad as it is exciting in an up-tempo number and it is no wonder that bandleaders and other artists inundated her with offers of recording work and live appearances.

In the immediate postwar period Ella was invited to work with the visionary impresario Norman Granz and she gratefully accepted a number of foreign tours with him. Following her release from a contract with Decca, she started to record for Granz's new jazz label, Verve, now undisputedly one of the finest jazz labels in existence. Ella was featured in numerous shows on television, as well as in a few feature films, while her live engagements rose to the heights of the Copacabana in New York City, the Hollywood Bowl and Carnegie Hall.

She is a lady of enormous charm and charisma whose total involvement in her artistry captivates the listener. She says her philosophy is to sing for herself in order that she can sing better for her audience and that it's always her intention to 'bring the little moments of happiness that everybody needs in their lives'. Her sense of rhythm is matched by a unique perception and ability to convey the essence of the lyrics and she has a marvellous talent for improvisation.

Norman Granz, impresario and recording mogul, took over as her manager and partnered her with Oscar Peterson, Louis Armstrong, Count Basie, Duke Ellington and others – the results were beyond compare. Listen to the track 'Summertime' on the *Get Into Jazz* CD or cassette to see what an excellent duo Ella Fitzgerald makes with Louis Armstrong.

Ella Fitzgerald is, for me, the First Lady of jazz singing. Although in the Eighties the timbre of her voice took on a more mature, harder edge, Ella Fitzgerald has produced an extensive recorded legacy which should be a part of the collection of anyone with the remotest interest in jazz.

RECOMMENDED LISTENING

At The Opera House
Verve: 831269-2 (CD)

Compact Jazz: Ella Fitzgerald Live
Verve: 833294-2 (CD)

Ella and Basie
Verve: 821576-2 (CD)

Ella and Louis (with Louis Armstrong)
Verve: 825373-2 (CD)

Ella and Louis Again, Volumes 1 and 2
Verve: 825374-2 (CD)

The Incomparable Ella
Polygram: 835 610-2 (CD)

The Songbooks
Verve: 823445-2 (CD)

Erroll Garner (1923(?)–77)
(piano)

Erroll Garner was born in Pittsburgh and the family moved to New York City just two years later. His father was a pianist but gave Erroll no formal musical training and young Erroll was therefore essentially self-taught. He claims he watched the family music teacher at work on the piano and picked up various techniques simply by looking and listening. He never learned to read music and so all his work was done by ear.

Garner developed a unique style that might well never have come about had he been subjected to a formal training in music, for he managed to create on the piano an extraordinary distinction between the roles of his two hands when playing. The left hand accomplished techniques which enabled him to sound like a self-contained rhythm section, while the right would play tunes and extemporize with such independence that the two hands could sound like two completely different people playing. He was a fine composer and arranger and he liked to incorporate unusual structures into his work, often having extended introductions or codas in his pieces. His most famous tune is 'Misty' – a classic standard that may well have been played, recorded and performed by more people than any other tune in the history of music. If any criticism can be levelled at Garner, the established jazz fraternity have sometimes frowned upon his music as being rather overtly commercial and, at times, a little too sentimental. That said, one cannot deny that he brought an enormous catalogue of wonderful tunes to the jazz scene as well as to mainstream, middle-of-the-road music and has thus crossed the boundaries of jazz and the commercial music world with an enviable degree of success.

One of the great characters of the jazz scene, Garner had a mischievous sense of humour and was enormously popular with his fellow musicians. He died at the age of fifty-five of a heart attack, having suffered from chronic emphysema for many years.

RECOMMENDED LISTENING

Body and Soul
Sony: 4679162 (CD)

Compact Jazz: Erroll Garner
Mercury: 830695 (CD)

Jazz Around Midnight – Erroll Garner
Verve: 846191 (CD)

Plays Gershwin & Kern
Mercury: 826224 (CD)

Soliloquy
CBS: 4656312 (CD)

Stan Getz (1927–91)
(tenor sax, soprano sax, baritone sax)

Stan Getz was born in Philadelphia and started his musical training playing the bass and the bassoon but quickly found the tenor saxophone more suited to the style of music that he wanted to play. He left school at the age of sixteen and, just one year later, started playing with Jack Teagarden's Big Band, before becoming a member of the Stan Kenton Band. He stayed for only a year and then moved around, working with a number of groups but mainly playing with Benny Goodman, Jimmy Dorsey, Randy Brooks and Herbie Field, before finally settling into a regular job with the Woody Herman 'Herd' in September 1947. He became known as one of the celebrated 'Four Brothers' through the recording of the tune of that name, which was later adopted as the signature tune for the Herman Band of that era. The other three brothers were Zoot Sims, Serge Chaloff and Herbie Stewart (later Al Cohn). The arrangements that featured the Four Brothers showed how well four saxophones in close harmony can sound – a device that was picked up by many arrangers thereafter.

Getz had always considered himself a bebop player and had even formed his own band called 'Stan Getz and His Bebop Boys' shortly before joining the Herman band. Getz certainly made a cool sound that was distinctive –

his first big break came through his performance on the 1948 recording of the tune 'Early Autumn' with the Herman band; this recording opened the jazz world's eyes to a new style of expressive sax playing that was in stark contrast to that of Charlie Parker and Coleman Hawkins, who had hitherto been the major trend-setters. From this time on Getz, known as 'The Sound', became a star of international standing.

In the early Fifties he undertook a number of tours in Europe, fronting his own quintet (sometimes quartet), and was particularly popular in Scandinavia where, in 1955, he was taken seriously ill through taking hard drugs. The year before he had been completely out of circulation owing to drug offences and this particular incident very nearly killed him. He had to remain in Copenhagen for some months in order to recover and this was followed by a period of convalescence in Sweden and in Africa, during which time he did not play at all. One year later he was invited to appear in the movie *The Benny Goodman Story* and began playing regularly again in Norman Granz's Jazz at the Philharmonic series.

A trip to South America in 1961 stimulated his existing interest in Latin music and he was particularly intrigued by the bossa nova and samba dance rhythms. With the guitarist Charlie Byrd, Getz had enormous fun creating a new jazz sound, producing the album *Jazz Samba*, and, just a year or so later, Getz collaborated with the Brazilian singer/guitarist Joao Gilberto and his wife Astrud to record songs like 'The Girl From Ipanema' and 'Desafinado' which quickly became huge commercial hits.

Getz played superbly right up until his death in 1991, despite severe health problems. Undoubtedly one of the great 'poets' on the tenor sax, he could really make the instrument talk. He was also a great source of encouragement and inspiration to young, up-and-coming jazz musicians whose careers he helped enormously. Gary Burton, Chick Corea, Stanley Clarke and Steve Swallow all fall into this category and it's interesting to note here a quote from Getz when talking about his desire to help other players: 'The two capital things are love and an open spirit, an openness towards other musicians and towards oneself and the world which surrounds us. One cannot behave like a horse with blinkers. One must open oneself to life, to music . . .' This receptive, open attitude to life and music is clearly demonstrated in Stan Getz's gift for presenting music in all kinds of styles – he considered himself to be an out-and-out bebop musician, but ended as one of the most accessible jazz players performing Latin jazz, so that even people who thought they didn't like jazz found themselves really enjoying it.

Recommended Listening

Compact/Walkman Jazz: Stan Getz And Friends
Verve: 835317-2 (CD)

Getz and Gilberto
Verve: 810048-2 (CD)

Jazz Samba
Verve: 810061-2 (CD)

Line For Lyons
Sonet: SNTCD 899 (CD)

Dizzy Gillespie (1917–93)
(trumpet, percussion, piano, vocals)

John Birks 'Dizzy' Gillespie was born in Cheraw, South Carolina, the son of an amateur musician and grew up in a respectable, happy, family environment. Although it was a period when racial discrimination was rife, this proved not to be a problem for Gillespie – he had a strength of character that enabled him to overcome any difficulties on this front. Other musicians, black ones in particular, were less fortunate and found such problems harder to overcome, but Gillespie will always be remembered for his role as an ambassador, later in life, when he smoothed the path for many poor young musicians who were endeavouring to forge their way into the music business.

Gillespie's father taught him to play a number of musical instruments but it was not until Dizzy was fourteen years old that he finally took up the trumpet. His father was extremely supportive of Dizzy's attraction to jazz and it was decided very early on that music would be his career. In 1937, at the age of twenty, Dizzy took his first professional job as the lead trumpeter in the Teddy Hill Band. He took over from his great idol, Roy Eldridge, and enjoyed touring Europe with musicians whom he'd always held in high regard. A few years later he joined the Cab Calloway Band and, while in New York, he sat in with a number of bands in the 52nd Street jazz clubs where he met Charlie Parker, Thelonious Monk and Kenny Clarke. His two-year stint in the Calloway Band was not the happiest of times for him – Gillespie and Calloway never really got on and their relationship came to an end when a fight broke out between the two at a club in Hartford and Dizzy pulled a knife on Calloway and cut him.

Musically, although he had always wanted to play swing jazz like his hero Eldridge, he never felt totally comfortable playing in this style. However, with Parker, Monk and Clarke, Gillespie found a voice that rang true in his heart and these four musicians really gave birth to the style of jazz known as bebop (or bop), one of the most important influences on everything that was to follow. In 1943 Charlie Parker and Dizzy Gillespie played alongside each other in Earl Hines's band and the following year they moved over to work with Billy Eckstine – they were almost inseparable. Soon 52nd Street became known as 'The Street of Bop' and it was here that Gillespie and Parker set new standards. Their first recordings were made in 1944 and from then on other musicians emulated their style. Dizzy loved to be out at the front entertaining the crowds and in 1945 formed his own big band, which he took on tour throughout Europe. The Paris concert of this tour made an especially big impact, illustrating clearly Gillespie's dynamism and innovative approach to jazz. He was fascinated by Afro-Cuban rhythms and the addition of Cuban drummer Chano Pozo to his band fuelled the world's interest in this genre. Tunes from this era included such classics as 'Manteca' and 'Tin Tin Deo' which were recorded on the Verve label in the early Sixties.

Gillespie was a truly remarkable character who was a natural entertainer. He was a marvellously talented 'scat' singer and comedian, as well as one of the most outstanding trumpet virtuosi ever. His phenomenal technique lent itself well to bebop jazz and one of the most amazing examples of his playing is to be found on the CD and cassette *Get Into Jazz*, where he is heard playing with Charlie Parker on the tune 'Leap Frog'. Very few have equalled his ability to play at such speed and with such expression. This recording was made in 1950 at around the time that the hardened jazz critics felt that both Gillespie and Parker had 'sold out' to the commercial world by recording albums featuring themselves as soloists to a backdrop of lush string arrangements. Gillespie wisely paid no heed to the critics and carried on his own way, knowing that even if the album had bordered on the overtly commercial, many found it immensely enjoyable and he had made some good money out of the project! A remarkable achievement in jazz.

One of the great ambassadors of jazz, Dizzy Gillespie fronted a new big band, organized by Quincy Jones, that toured Pakistan, Lebanon, Syria, Turkey, Yugoslavia and Greece from March to May 1956. This venture was funded by the US State Department and was the first time the United States government had provided financial aid to a jazz-based project. The tour was such a success that Gillespie kept the band together in one form or another until 1958, taking it on tours to Latin America and the Soviet Union. Later in the Seventies he toured extensively throughout the high school and college campus scene and in 1978 he was invited by President Jimmy Carter to perform at the White House.

On a more personal note, Dizzy Gillespie was a devout member of the Baha'i faith from 1968 and held very close to his heart the faith's ideals of world peace and world unity. He died at the beginning of 1993, leaving his mark both as a true 'citizen of the world' and also as one of the greatest entertainers and innovators in the history of jazz.

Recommended Listening

Bird and Diz
Verve: 831133-2 (CD)

Compact Jazz: Dizzy Gillespie – Big Band
Verve: 314511393-2 (CD)

Compact/Walkman Jazz: Dizzy Gillespie
Mercury: 832574-2 (CD/cassette)

Diz and Getz
Verve: 833559-2 (CD)

Dizzy Gillespie and The Double Six of Paris
Philips: 830224-2 (CD)

Dizzy in Paris
Vogue: 6556 19 (CD)

Dizzy's Diamonds
Verve: 513875-2 (CD)

Duets with Sonny Rollins and Sonny Stitt
Verve: 835674-2 (CD)

The Legendary Big Band Concert 1948
GNP: 6556 12 (CD)

Shaw 'Nuff
Musicraft: MVSCD-53 (CD)

Benny Goodman (1909–86)
(clarinet)

Crowned the 'King of Swing', Benny Goodman was given this accolade for his immeasurable talent in that field. However, not only was he one of the finest exponents of swing clarinet playing, he was also an accomplished classical clarinettist who played Mozart, Brahms and Weber as well as many pieces that were either written especially for him (like the *Concerto* by Aaron Copland and *Contrasts* by Bartok), or were directly inspired by his playing.

He was born into a large, poor family in Chicago. His father was an immigrant Jewish tailor by trade, who gave young Benny a clarinet to experiment with at the age of eight so that the boy could join the synagogue band. By the age of ten he was already showing signs of being an extremely promising musician and just two years later was on stage in a talent contest with Benny Meroff, giving an imitation of the most eminent clarinettist of the day, Ted Lewis. Not surprisingly, Benjamin David Goodman won first prize and never looked back. He was just seventeen years old when he was sent for by the prominent talent scout Ben Pollack, who invited him to join the band at the Venice Ballroom in Los Angeles. Goodman quickly gained an excellent reputation and was soon fronting bands himself and taking the lead in a number of recordings. By 1934 Goodman had also spent some time in New York and been constantly in demand both as a session musician and for live engagements. He formed his own band in the spring of 1934 and had a regular spot on NBC as part of the extremely popular show 'Let's Dance'. He later took the band out on tour but first reactions were not wildly enthusiastic. By the time the band had made its way round to Los Angeles, however, people had become familiar with the recordings and Benny Goodman's band received a rapturous reception. This was without doubt the start of the swing band era.

The next two years saw Goodman's band go from strength to strength. He introduced black musicians into his own previously 'white' band and brought in such superlative talents as Gene Krupa on drums, the singer Helen Ward and the pianists Jess Stacy and Teddy Wilson. Throughout the next eight to ten years, Benny Goodman's band stayed at the very top of the swing band tree, recording and touring widely. Goodman took the decision to slow down in 1951 and made only occasional appearances with small groups thereafter, except for one tour with a big band in 1953.

The film *The Benny Goodman Story* was made in Hollywood in 1955 and was nothing like the commercial or artistic success it should have been. One of the best things that came about as a result of the project was that Goodman formed a band especially for the movie and kept it going for a few years, notably on tours to the Far East, the Soviet Union (his was the first jazz band ever to tour there) and one around the United States. He appeared in a number of other movies, none of which is considered to be more than light-hearted entertainment.

Goodman's style in jazz was well crafted. He had a fine technique on the instrument and this, coupled with his extensive knowledge of harmony and rhythm, led to a highly stylized idiom of soloing that set several trends for all jazz clarinettists who followed him. He had a wonderful sense of phrasing and was able to play extended flourishes of highly ornamented notes. Among his best-known tracks are 'Stompin' at the Savoy', 'Blue Skies', 'Let's Dance' and 'Sing, Sing, Sing'.

RECOMMENDED LISTENING

Benny Rides Again
MCA: 31264 (CD)

B. G. In Hi-Fi
Capitol: CDP 7926842 (CD)

The Birth Of Swing (1935–1936)
RCA Bluebird: ND 90601 (3CD)

Compact Jazz: Benny Goodman
Verve: 820543 (CD)

Let's Dance
Big Band Era: 260 1792 (CD)

Dexter Gordon (1923–89)
(tenor sax, soprano sax)

Another giant of the tenor saxophone, Dexter Gordon was born in Los Angeles in 1923 and, hailing from the stable led by Coleman Hawkins, was himself extremely influential in developing the styles of artists like Stan Getz, John Coltrane and Sonny Stitt.

Gordon took up music as a young boy, playing both the soprano and tenor saxophones with equal proficiency, though ultimately it was the tenor for which he was particularly renowned. His career started at seventeen, when he was invited to join the Lionel Hampton Band. This was a major break for the young Gordon and over the next twenty years or so he worked in many famous bands, such as those led by Fletcher Henderson, Louis Armstrong and Billy Eckstine.

In 1945 he moved to New York where he met and worked with Charlie Parker and freelanced with considerable success, also making a number of recordings under his own name. From this time on his drug-taking made him much less reliable and inevitably had significant consequences – two years in prison on drugs charges certainly took their toll. He later moved to Copenhagen, making occasional visits back to the United States and to festivals around Europe.

Gordon had a wide following and his engaging style of playing won him many fans. Also an extremely talented actor, he appeared in several films, perhaps the most famous of which are *The Connection* and *Round Midnight*. In the latter film, he was nominated for an Oscar for his portrayal of a burned-out, down-trodden musician.

His recordings on the Blue Note label come highly recommended, particularly the album *Ballads* which sees him in fine form.

Ballads
Blue Note: CDP 7 96579-2 (CD)

More Than You Know
Steeplechase: 1030 (CD/LP/cassette)

Our Man In Paris
Blue Note: CDP 7463942 (CD)

A Swingin' Affair
Blue Note: CDP 7841332 (CD)

Stephane Grappelli (born 1908)
(violin)

Stephane Grappelli has captured the imagination of music lovers all over the world during the last fifty years as the best-known mainstream jazz violinist. He was born and raised by his father in Paris, living in poor circumstances, which were significantly improved when he won a scholarship to study at the Paris Conservatoire. He later became a member of the celebrated Quintette du Hot-Club de France and, with Django Reinhardt, was a driving force in the French and European jazz movement.

He started by busking in the streets and progressed to being a cinema musician, playing in jazz cafés and accompanying silent movies in Paris. He moved to London and spent some considerable time playing with such musicians as George Shearing, Fats Waller, Duke

Ellington and, of course, the guitarist Django Reinhardt, with whom he is most closely associated. Their famous 'Quintette' was formed in 1934 and after a gap in the early Forties the two got together again to record a swing version of 'La Marseillaise', which they titled 'Echoes of France'. Grappelli has played all over the world and has featured at all the main international festivals and major concert halls, as well as on numerous television and radio programmes.

From the time of Reinhardt's death in 1953, Grappelli travelled extensively, doing mainly commercial work as the jazz clubs' interest in him had waned somewhat. However, in 1972 the British-based guitarist Diz Disley invited Grappelli to Britain to tour the local folk clubs in a quartet that also featured Denny Wright on guitar and John Hawkesworth on bass. This was a great success and really put Grappelli back on the map; he collaborated with such diverse artists as Oscar Peterson, Martial Solal, Yehudi Menuhin, Gary Burton, Joe Venuti and Barney Kessel – there are numerous recordings of these collaborations that are well worth exploring. His partnership with the highly talented guitarist Martin Taylor has also produced some excellent work and the great man appears to go from strength to strength.

RECOMMENDED LISTENING

Compact Jazz: Stephane Grappelli
MPS Jazz: 831370-2 (CD)

Jealousy
CFP: CDB 767 113-2 (CD)

Parisian Thoroughfare
Black Lion: BLP 60132 (CD/LP/cassette)

Quintette du Hot-Club de France
Vogue: VGCD 60070 (CD)

Special Stephane Grappelli (1947–61)
EMI: CZ 317 (CD)

Lionel Hampton (born 1909)
(vibraphone, piano, drums, vocals)

Born in Louisville and raised in Chicago, Lionel Hampton started his musical career as a drummer in the Chicago Defender Boys' Band. His family moved to California when he was nineteen years old and Lionel was soon invited to play alongside some of the most eminent jazz musicians including Les Hite, Eddie Barefield and in the Paul Howard Orchestra. His first really big break came when Louis Armstrong (who was at that time fronting the Les Hite Band) asked if anyone knew how to play the vibraphone – Hampton had never touched one before in his life, but with youthful enthusiasm said that he did. After a short audition for Armstrong, in which Hampton played one of the great trumpeter's solos note for note on the vibes, Armstrong was suitably impressed by the young man's versatility and proceeded to record a beautiful version of the tune 'Memories of You' with him, bringing

Hampton's unique gift to the attention of the whole jazz world.

Lionel Hampton stayed with the Hite Band for another four years until he decided to form his own group, which was engaged at Sebastian's Cotton Club in Los Angeles. Benny Goodman heard him at the club and immediately invited him to record with him and to join his quartet alongside Gene Krupa and Teddy Wilson. This combination of talents proved extremely successful and among the many highlights of their time together was the Carnegie Hall concert in 1938, which received unanimous critical and audience acclaim.

From about 1940 Hampton was given the freedom of the RCA Victor studios and fronted numerous recordings with various pick-up bands, featuring such giants from the jazz world as Dizzy Gillespie, Earl Hines, Johnny Hodges, Coleman Hawkins and Ben Webster. These recordings (more than sixty were made) have now become collectors' items. Hampton formed his own big band at this time, made the famous recording 'Flyin' Home' in 1942 and has gone on to lead bands and tour extensively ever since. From the early Fifties he also recorded a number of albums for the Verve label and there are numerous recordings featuring Hampton both as a vibraphone player (as he is best known) and as a drummer and pianist.

RECOMMENDED LISTENING

Chicago Jazz Concert
CBS: 21107 (CD)

Compact Jazz: Lionel Hampton
Verve: 833 287-2 (CD)

Hamp's Blues
LRC CD: 7973 (CD)

Just Jazz
MCA: 42329 (CD)

Live At The Blue Note
Telarc Jazz: CD-83308 (CD)

Herbie Hancock (born 1940)
(piano, keyboards)

Herbie Hancock was born in Chicago and right from the very start he was destined for a career in the music business, although in his early days it was thought that this would be as a classical concert pianist. Regarded as a child prodigy, he gave his first performance of Mozart's Piano Concerto in D major with the Chicago Symphony Orchestra at the astonishingly young age of eleven.

However, it soon became clear that his real interest lay in jazz music and from his middle teens he started transcribing many of the solos of Oscar Peterson in order to play them himself at home. His classical background and formal training have stood him in good stead, for he is now regarded as one of the most gifted of contemporary keyboard players, alongside Keith Jarrett and Chick Corea. His playing has a beautifully refined quality in terms of both the sound that he produces on the piano and his remarkable technical facility that makes even the most complex writing sound effortless.

Hancock made his way to New York in the late Fifties and worked with artists like Coleman Hawkins and later with Miles Davis, who invited him to join his famous new quintet in 1963. He signed a record deal with Blue Note Records at this time and released some highly influential material, including the album *Taking Off*, which became a big hit. He was at the forefront of the development of jazz during this period and was instrumental in the transition of what may be called modern jazz through to jazz rock and electro-jazz rock. His command of synthesizers and hi-tech recording techniques employing effect units made a big impact and, when he formed his own group in the late Sixties, he attracted a huge following which has, by and large, stayed with him through a number of stylistic developments.

In 1982 he formed a new quartet with Tony Williams, Ron Carter and the virtuoso trumpeter Wynton Marsalis that toured throughout Europe and Japan to great critical acclaim. His later move back to electronic music in the mid-Eighties led to co-writing a tune called 'Rockit' which provided the inspiration for an award-winning video that made the album *Future Shock* into a smash hit all over the world. Hancock now has a band called VSOP and plays in a piano duo with Chick Corea.

RECOMMENDED LISTENING

Best of Herbie Hancock (2) (The Blue Note Years)
Blue Note: BNZ 143 (CD)

An Evening with Herbie Hancock & Chick Corea
CBS: 4664422 (CD)

A Jazz Collection
Columbia: 4679012 (CD)

Maiden Voyage
Blue Note: 743392 (CD)

Takin' Off
Blue Note: 746506 (CD)

Coleman Hawkins (1901–69)
(tenor sax, vocals)

Born in St Joseph, Missouri, Hawkins started his musical
life on the piano and the 'cello. He took up the saxophone
at the age of nine and like many of his contemporaries in
Missouri quickly became active in the local boys' bands
in Kansas City. He was spotted at an early stage in his
career by the legendary blues singer, Mamie Smith, with
whom he was invited to tour as part of her backing group,
The Jazz Hounds, between 1921 and 1923. After this tour
he settled in New York, still playing for Mamie Smith
and freelancing with a variety of jazz units, including that
of Fletcher Henderson. Hawkins earned high respect from
everyone he worked with and quickly became the first
really famous tenor sax player. He moved to England in
1934 and then went on to tour Europe, performing and
recording with a fascinating mixture of bands, including
those fronted by Jack Hylton, Michel Warlop, Benny
Carter, Django Reinhardt and George Chisholm.

He returned to the United States in 1939 where he formed his own band and later that year recorded the tune 'Body and Soul' for Blue Note Records – it has since become an all-time favourite for many. He formed his own sixteen-piece band but soon gave that up to get into the bebop scene, playing in smaller combo bands. He enjoyed this kind of lifestyle, touring around all the big jazz festivals in the United States and Europe.

Coleman Hawkins (or 'Bean' as he became known) was the principal innovator who had a significant influence on all saxophone players until the time Lester Young hit the scene. His sound was rich, warm and full-toned, while his power of expression remained unsurpassed until Lester Young and Stan Getz developed the starkly contrasting 'cool' sound of the tenor.

Recommended Listening

Body And Soul
RCA Bluebird: ND 85717 (CD/LP/cassette)

Coleman Hawkins 1934–1937
Jazz Classics: CLASSICS 602 (CD)

Compact Jazz: Coleman Hawkins and Ben Webster
Verve: 833296 (CD/cassette)

The Hawk In Europe
ASV: AJA 5054 (CD)

Wrapped Tight
Impulse!: GRP 11092 (CD/cassette)

Woody Herman (1913–87)
(clarinet, alto sax, vocals)

Born in Milwaukee, Woody Herman was active as an entertainer from a very early age, singing and dancing in local theatres and music halls. He started learning the saxophone at the age of nine and went on to play in all sorts of bands and in every popular style imaginable. He moved around in the Thirties, playing with a number of bands, including Isham Jones Juniors for Decca; when that band broke up, he put together a co-operative band that cut the single 'The Woodchopper's Ball' which sold over a million copies. This orchestra played what the public wanted to hear, which was a mixture of fast bluesy numbers, pop songs and middle-of-the-road Dixieland favourites.

Herman effected a major change of personnel between 1943 and 1944, bringing in a number of more serious musicians to create a band that went on to have its own radio show and win numerous awards. The music it performed was far removed from the more commercial sounds of the previous period and, throughout the next ten years, Herman's band developed a reputation for creating music that satisfied the purist jazz lovers as well as a wider general public. His sidemen included such enormous talents as Zoot Sims, Stan Getz and Al Cohn. The band that was together between 1947 and 1949 became known as The Four Brothers, the later band being known as The Herd.

Throughout the Fifties and Sixties, Herman developed the sound of the big band still further, always adhering to the traditional format but introducing a more modern repertoire that would not alienate his followers. Composers who contributed to the works performed by the Herman band included such diverse artists as Horace Silver, Thelonious Monk, John Coltrane and Herbie Hancock.

Woody Herman will be remembered for keeping big bands alive as well as for his great sense of vision for the future development of jazz.

RECOMMENDED LISTENING

At The Woodchoppers Ball
Dance Band Days: DBCD 09 (CD/cassette)

Best of the Big Bands
CBS: 4666212 (CD)

Compact/Walkman Jazz: Woody Herman
Verve: 835319 (CD/cassette)

The 40th Anniversary Carnegie Hall Concert
RCA Bluebird: ND 86878 (CD/cassette)

Keeper of the Flame
Capitol: CZ 505 (CD)

Earl 'Fatha' Hines (1903–83)
(piano, vocals)

Earl Kenneth ('Fatha') Hines came from a very musical family background, his father being a trumpeter in the Eureka Brass Band and his mother an organist. Earl was given piano lessons from the age of nine and soon decided that he would like to be a professional pianist – an ambition that he realized at the age of seventeen. He took a number of freelance jobs but soon settled into a full-time position with the singer Lois Deppe in Chicago, where he stayed for some years.

Many of the most famous jazz artists in Chicago wanted to work with Hines and undoubtedly his most celebrated collaboration was that with Louis Armstrong, with whom he featured in both the Hot Five and the Hot Seven. Hines developed a very distinctive style on the piano which was emulated by many who followed. He started at the time when 'stride piano' techniques were very much the fashion, but managed to create his own unique style that was way ahead of its time – he included 'stride' and 'walking' bass lines to accompany punchy single melodic lines in the right hand and employed many surprising musical devices such as trills, sudden silences and octave jumps that constantly delighted both the audiences and his fellow musicians.

As the bebop movement made its mark in the Forties, Hines also worked alongside such artists as Charlie Parker, Dizzy Gillespie, Benny Green, Benny Harris, Billy Eckstine and Sarah Vaughan. Among his most famous recordings are the tracks 'Deep Forest', 'My Monday

Date', 'Stormy Monday Blues' and 'I Got It Bad'.

He was undoubtedly one of the most formidable of pianists at this time and in the Forties he rejoined Armstrong as part of the Louis Armstrong All Stars. He was given the title 'Fatha' by a radio announcer who wished to award some form of accolade to Hines for his innovative approach to the instrument and to music in general – there was already a Duke, a King, so why not a Fatha!

RECOMMENDED LISTENING

Earl Fatha Hines (1928–1955)
Cleo: CLCD 5031 (CD)

Hangover Club (1956)
GNP Crescendo: 600189 (CD)

Piano Man
RCA Bluebird: NK/ND/NL 86750 (CD/LP/cassette)

Tour de Force
Black Lion: BLCD 760140 (CD)

Johnny Hodges (1907–70)
(alto sax, soprano sax)

Born in Cambridge, Massachusetts, Johnny Hodges first took up the drums and later the piano, finally picking up the saxophone in 1920 at the age of fourteen. He was essentially self-taught but took some lessons with the clarinettist and saxophonist Sidney Bechet, who presented him with a soprano sax in recognition of his great talent. Hodges played with a number of bands in the middle Twenties but had his big break in 1928 when he was invited to join the Duke Ellington Band, where he remained for nearly twenty-three years. During the early Thirties Hodges and Benny Carter, and to a lesser extent Willie Smith, reigned as the kings of the alto saxophone. Hodges had a warm, expressive sound; his vibrato and his ability to glissando from one note to another earned him the glowing title 'voice of the saxophone'.

When he left the Ellington band, Johnny Hodges formed his own band and in 1955 he worked in New York on a daily TV show but then went back to his old job in the Ellington band, preferring the financial security it provided and, indeed, the creative freedom. Hodges is widely recorded both with the Ellington band and with a number of solo artists who hired his services, including Lionel Hampton, Teddy Wilson and Cootie Williams.

Hodges was a charming man who was liked by all – he never liked to assert himself and was even reluctant to stand when taking a solo. This diffidence was also a major factor in his decision to go back to the ranks of the Ellington band and for that, we should be grateful – his contributions are quite superb.

RECOMMENDED LISTENING

Compact Jazz: Johnny Hodges – Wild Bill Davis
Verve: 839288 (CD)

Everybody Knows Johnny Hodges
Impulse!: GRP 11162 (CD)

In A Mellotone
Bluebird: ND 82305 (CD)

Rarities And Private Recordings
Suisa: JZCD 361 (CD)

Triple Play
Bluebird: ND 90208 (CD)

Billie Holiday (1915–59)
(vocals)

Born in Baltimore on 4 July 1915, Billie Holiday stands as one of the most gifted artists in the whole history of jazz. Her father, the banjo player Clarence Holiday, was just fifteen when she was born and by the time young Billie was ten he had left her and her mother absolutely penniless and with a very bleak future indeed. Despite the most harrowing personal problems very early in life, she managed to live and breathe music through her unique style of singing. She had a desperately unhappy childhood, being raped at the age of ten and drawn in to a prostitution racket, making her first inroads into the music business by singing in cabaret bars and clubs.

Soon she was the name on everyone's lips and was invited to work with Count Basie, Benny Goodman, Teddy Wilson, Artie Shaw and Louis Armstrong during her tragically brief career. She never learned to read music, which, surprisingly, never seemed to hamper her progress – she simply relied upon her natural talent and brought to every song a deeply committed and unique interpretation. Many have criticized the inherent quality of her voice, which to some people's ears sounds a little uncultured. However, no-one can deny that she brought an honesty and a depth of emotion to her singing that cannot fail to move her audience. There are numerous excellent recordings of her work, the best of which were made from the mid-Thirties throughout a ten-year period and these are well captured on disc.

She made friends with the saxophonist Lester Young and both fell victim to alcohol and drug abuse. Holiday seemed hell-bent on a course of self-destruction, drinking heavily and taking sedatives at the same time. As the years went on her voice certainly suffered the detrimental effects of such abuse. She was imprisoned in 1947 on narcotics charges and when released was banned from appearing in New York clubs, thereafter only giving concert performances and undertaking recording engagements.

Before she died in 1959, at the age of forty-four, her autobiography, *Lady Sings The Blues*, was published; a film of it was made in 1972, starring Diana Ross in the title role. The title implies that Holiday was an out-and-out blues singer but this is not really the case, for although her early influences included the great blues singer Bessie Smith, Holiday herself rarely sang true blues, preferring to be considered a serious jazz artist who used the voice as an expressive instrument. Throughout her career, during which she recorded some 270 songs, only three bona fide blues tracks feature, and the stylistic traits of obligatory flattened 'blue notes' and adherence to twelve-bar and thirty-two bar chord structures do not in any way predominate. It's a point that has been the source of much discussion amongst jazz historians and critics – most of them come to the conclusion that Holiday was a jazz singer, per se, and that the classification of 'blues singer' emanates from the marketing men surrounding her recording career and people wishing to put a 'tag' on the books and films about her life.

The life came tragically to an end after a concert at the Phoenix Theatre in New York, when she was taken to hospital with severe narcotic addiction problems. While actually on her deathbed, she was arrested on a drugs charge – a suitably dramatic if macabre ending to one of the most influential singers in the history of jazz.

RECOMMENDED LISTENING

Compact Jazz: Billie Holiday
Verve: 831371-2 (CD)

Her Transitional Years 1933–1950 Volume 1
Jazzmen 62550001 (CD)

Lady Day and Prez 1937–1941
Giants of Jazz: GOJCD 0218 (CD)

The Legacy (1933–1958)
Columbia: 47724 (CD/cassette)

Keith Jarrett (born 1945)
(piano)

One of the most important figures in the contemporary music scene, Keith Jarrett stands at the very pinnacle of achievement in the music industry having been part of many of the most influential developments in the last twenty years.

He was born in Allentown, Pennsylvania on 8 May 1945 into a musically aware family; both his mother and father were involved in amateur local orchestras and choirs. Keith Jarrett was a precocious child in every sense, he was talking before his first birthday and showed an extraordinary ability on the piano from the age of three, being able to copy tunes he heard on the radio and showing an enormous gift for playing by ear. He gave his first concert at the age of six and progressed rapidly. His formal studies began at the celebrated academy for jazz musicians, the Berklee School of Music in Boston, but he was expelled before the end of his first year for playing the strings from the inside of the piano – a technique for which he is now renowned!

He moved to New York in 1964 and tried to earn a living as a pianist but times were hard – he was forever moving from apartment to apartment, all of which had mice, cockroaches and unsavoury neighbours who did not appreciate his constant piano practice. He worked as an occasional session musician doing jingles and commercial work – a scene he was not at all keen on. At this time he played drums as well as keyboards and sat in with jazz groups whenever it was possible. One night at the Village

Vanguard he was playing in a small combo and Art Blakey was at the bar listening – Jarrett was immediately asked to join Art's group, The New Jazz Messengers, but he stayed only for a few months as the conditions under which the group had to work and tour did not suit him. The band was expected to travel across the United States from coast to coast, each member taking turns at driving the car, which had to house the band, the manager and the instruments!

Jarrett was soon after invited to join the Charles Lloyd Quartet, with whom he spent three or four very stimulating years developing his style. During this period he formed his own trio with Paul Motian on drums and Charlie Haden on bass and together they gave numerous concerts and made some excellent records. Shortly after his twenty-fifth birthday, Jarrett was invited to play with Miles Davis, initially as the second keyboardist to Chick Corea, but later as the principal player. This was a most important time and one when the great Miles Davis was instrumental in transforming the history of jazz. Keith Jarrett was very much a part of that movement and two recordings from this time (spring/summer 1970), *Live Evil* and *Miles at the Fillmore*, represent landmarks in the turning point of the jazz rock era.

Jarrett has been extensively recorded on the ECM label, as a soloist and with his various smaller combos. He formed a small band called Belonging with the Norwegian saxophonist Jan Garbarek and this has also produced some fascinating work on disc. In the last ten years Keith Jarrett has been involved in numerous projects, forever touring the world and giving concerts to capacity houses. He has a stage presence that is second to none and captivates his audience in his extended improvisatory pieces that demonstrate not only his phenomenal technical prowess but an overwhelming depth of musicality and an ability to construct intricate pieces that are truly hypnotic. He has also recorded many classical works, most recently an unusual but absorbing interpretation of the complete Preludes and Fugues for solo piano by Dmitri Shostakovich.

Keith Jarrett is certainly one of the most significant jazz musicians at work in the Nineties and his catalogue of recordings is well worth exploring.

RECOMMENDED LISTENING

Belonging
ECM: 1050 (CD/LP/cassette)

Changes
ECM: 1276 (CD/LP)

The Cure (New York, April 1990)
ECM: 1440 (CD/LP/cassette)

Expectations
Columbia: 467902 (CD)

The Köln Concert
ECM: 1064/5 (CD/LP/cassette)

Standards: Volume 1
ECM: 1255 (CD/LP/cassette)

Standards: Volume 2
ECM: 1289 (CD/LP)

Freddie Keppard (1890–1933)
(trumpet, cornet)

Freddie Keppard was one of the true New Orleans jazz musicians born at the turn of the century – at the very time when jazz was evolving in the southern states of America. As with many children in New Orleans at this time, music was a part of his culture; Freddie was given a trumpet to play almost as soon as he could walk and he soon found himself performing with the Olympia Brass Band, of which he later became the leader. He was a member of the Original Creole Orchestra and left New Orleans in 1913 to go on tour with this band, becoming their leader in 1915.

Moving to Chicago, he gave up life on the road and settled down and formed his own band, as well as playing with artists like Ollie Powers, Erskine Tate and King Oliver. He was a very sickly man and contracted tuberculosis which finally killed him in 1933 at the comparatively young age of forty-four. Sadly, although his band was among the very first to be invited to make a record, Keppard turned down the opportunity and never had the sort of career for which he might otherwise have been destined. Consequently there are no solo album recordings of Keppard's work, but he can be heard with his Jazz Cardinals band and Cook's Dreamland Orchestra on an LP shared with the Red Onion Jazz Babies (Fountain FJ-107).

Gene Krupa (1909–73)
(drums)

Eugene 'Gene' Krupa was born in Chicago, Illinois and started playing the drums as a schoolboy when he also formally studied percussion. His first important work came in 1927 when he was asked to make a recording with the McKenzie–Condon Chicagoans and these sessions were apparently the first ever to employ a bass drum in the recording. He worked in and around Chicago at this time, but never really made any impact, so in 1929 he moved to New York where he immediately found success playing with Red Nichols at the Hollywood Restaurant. His reputation grew very quickly and he was soon invited to play on numerous recordings, notably those with Bix Beiderbecke and Benny Goodman. The latter was so impressed with Krupa's work that he asked him to join his big band and, following the outstanding success of his work on the best-selling recording of the tune 'Sing, Sing, Sing', Gene Krupa found international fame and soon afterwards formed his own band.

In 1942, Krupa reached a low point in his career when he was arrested for possession of marijuana and had to serve a brief jail sentence. He kept in touch with as many people as possible and specifically maintained his contact with Benny Goodman. He undertook occasional tours with Goodman's big band as well with Tommy Dorsey and as part of Norman Granz's Jazz at the Philharmonic extravaganza. In 1959 a film entitled *The Gene Krupa Story* was made; this was one of the most inaccurate and fictitious screenplays in history – Krupa recorded the soundtrack, but the title role was taken by an actor named Sal Mineo.

Krupa was a marvellous showman and earned the respect of his fellow musicians, even though the critics were prone to describe his style as forceful and lacking in subtlety – it was this very dynamism and strength in his playing that made him unique. It is even reported that Krupa was the one drummer that Buddy Rich never put down! Krupa stands alongside Buddy Rich as one of the finest white jazz drummers in the history of jazz.

Recommended Listening

Benny Goodman and His Orchestra (1935–39)
Giants of Jazz: GOJCD 53042 (CD)

Birth of the Swing
Bluebird: ND 90601(3) (CD)

Compact Jazz: Gene Krupa
Verve: 833286 (CD)

Compact Jazz: Gene Krupa and Buddy Rich
Verve: 835314 (CD)

Drummin' Man
Charly: CDCharly 81 (CD)

Cleo Laine (born 1927)
(vocals)

One of Britain's most distinctive and best-loved jazz singers, Clementina Dinah Campbell Laine first made her mark when she appeared with the Johnny Dankworth Seven and Big Band in the Fifties. She fell in love with the bandleader and the couple have each earned the greatest respect for their talents in what have been highly succssful careers.

Cleo is widely known for her jazz and middle-of-the-road singing and her unique style of improvisation, but in the early Sixties she also developed a serious reputation as a singer in musicals, with appearances in such shows as *The Seven Deadly Sins, Show Boat* and *Colette*, and as a straight actress in several roles for both the stage and television.

In more recent years she has undertaken a number of tours – she is particularly popular in the United States – as well as performing at the Festival at the family home in Wavendon. Her occasional appearances on British television have always been well received and she stands as one of the most popular jazz singers of the last fifty years. There are numerous recordings of her work available, some of which certainly cannot be considered bona fide jazz recordings, but which have given Cleo Laine considerable commercial success in the last twenty years or so – *Sometimes When We Touch*, recorded with the flautist James Galway, is one such example.

Cleo at Carnegie
DRG (USA): CDXP 2101 (CD)

Jazz
RCA: RD 60548 (CD)

One More Day
DRG (USA): CDSL 5198 (CD)

Sometimes When We Touch
RCA: RD 83628 (CD)

Word Songs
Philips: 8304612 (CD)

Humphrey Lyttelton (born 1921)
(trumpet, cornet, clarinet)

Born in Windsor on 23 May 1921, Humphrey Lyttelton
is well known both as one of the most celebrated British
bandleaders and as a broadcaster, author and all-round
commentator on the subject of jazz.

His father was a housemaster at Eton, where 'Humph'
became a pupil and had his first taste of jazz music. So
inspired was he that he decided to teach himself to
play the cornet. National conscription took him into the
Grenadier Guards, but by 1947 Lyttelton was ready and
eager to become a professional musician and was immediately enlisted into George Webb's Dixieland Band.
He then formed his own band which a year or so later had

developed such a reputation that in 1949 the band was engaged to accompany the legendary Sidney Bechet. Lyttelton was obviously destined for great things and although his musical instincts were firmly allied to trad jazz at a time when the style was immensely popular, Lyttelton moved on to develop a style all of his own.

He enlarged the size of his band to an octet and created a sound not dissimilar to that of the Ellington Band of the late Thirties, encompassing a good feel for dance band jazz along the way. He replaced the traditional banjo in the band with a guitarist and also brought in an alto saxophonist. Such moves brought inevitable criticism from the mainstream jazz fraternity, but Lyttelton enjoyed the praise and adulation of a large and loyal following. His roots were obviously in the sound of the New Orleans and Chicago bands and his own style of trumpet playing derived much inspiration from Louis Armstrong, but in time he moved on to incorporate a very wide-ranging repertoire.

In 1956 he had a hit in the British charts with the quartet version of 'Bad Penny Blues'. This put him very much on the map in commercial terms and he capitalized on it by bringing into the band a celebrated trio of saxophonists to enhance the sound of his arrangements – Tony Coe, Jimmy Skidmore and Joe Temperley made a big impact on the overall sound of the band and proved a very popular addition. His numerous collaborations with the singer Helen Shapiro, both in the recording studio and in live concerts, proved to be a marvellous partnership, enabling the band to perform much of the old Ellington material that Ella Fitzgerald had done with the Duke's band. Shapiro was also superb in popular standards and these were always among the favourites of Lyttelton's audience, though not always in the true jazz tradition.

Lyttelton is also a renowned broadcaster and the author of a number of fine books which give enormous insight into the British jazz scene as a whole – *I Play As I Please* and *Second Chorus* were published in the mid-Fifties and feature his own illustrations, perhaps inspired by the clarinettist-cartoonist Wally Fawkes whom Lyttelton had engaged in his own band back in the late Forties. He has also written a series of books for Robson Books entitled *The Best of Jazz*; they contain biographies and a wonderful picture of jazz in the Twenties and Thirties.

RECOMMENDED LISTENING

Beano Boogie
Calligraph: CLGCD 021 (CD/LP/cassette)

Echoes of the Duke
Calligraph: CLGCD 002 (CD)

Humph 'n' Helen
Calligraph: CLGCD 025 (CD)

Jazz At The Royal Festival Hall/Jazz At The Conway Hall
Dormouse: DM22 (CD)

The Parlophone Years
Dormouse: DM21 (CD)

Glenn Miller (1904–44)
(trombone, arranger)

Although not recognized as a fine jazz player himself – he was a distinctly ordinary trombonist – Glenn Miller is world renowned as one of the most popular big band leaders of all time. He was born Alton Glenn Miller in Clarinda, Iowa on 1 March 1904 and studied music at Colorado University but he was not cut out for academic study and failed miserably. He always enjoyed playing in bands but showed his real talent as an arranger with his first exploits on the semi-professional circuit with the Henry Pollack band. His gift in this direction became well known and he was soon invited to arrange for shows like *Strike Up The Band* and *Girl Crazy*, as well as doing numerous smaller jobs for music on the radio.

A number of freelance jobs followed (with brief flirtations as a singer) until he was invited to be the musical director of the film star Smith Ballew's dance band. Miller seized the opportunity with both hands and quickly became a strict and proficient bandleader of the first order. His arrangements were imaginative and well liked but it may have been by chance that he hit upon the elusive 'sound' for which he has become famous. His lead trumpeter, the virtuoso Pee Wee Erwin, asked to play the lead alto sax parts on the trumpet and Miller agreed; however, when Erwin was not available and less able players had to play the parts, Miller handed them over to the clarinet chair instead. The result was the inimitable sound that we have come to know and love on tracks like 'Moonlight Serenade'.

Throughout the early Forties Glenn Miller enjoyed huge commercial success with a string of hits including 'Chattanooga-choo-choo', 'In The Mood' and 'Pennsylvania 65000'. His life came to a tragic end in 1944, when he flew out to Paris ahead of the band to ensure that all was in order for his concerts there, his plane disappeared and a year later he was officially pronounced dead.

This tragic loss was sorely felt by the musical world at the time but his music lives on, enjoyed by a very wide audience both on record and through live performances by bands like the Syd Lawrence Orchestra. He can never be classed as a truly significant contributor to mainstream jazz but equally he cannot be ignored since his jazz-based big band arrangements have achieved such phenomenal popularity the world over.

RECOMMENDED LISTENING

The Genius of Glenn Miller
RCA: ND 90090 (CD)

The Genius of Glenn Miller Volume 2
RCA: ND 90205 (CD)

The Glenn Miller Story
Deja Vu: DVRECD 06 (CD)

String Of Pearls
Complete Record Co. Ltd: BSTCD 9107 (CD)

Charles Mingus (1922–79)
(double bass, piano)

Charles Mingus was a renowned bass player, composer and bandleader, who first made a name for himself at the beginning of the bebop era. He was born in Nogales in Arizona and spent his childhood in the ghetto of Watts in Los Angeles. His two older sisters learned the piano and while young Charles was at school he started his own musical training on the trombone, later switching to the 'cello and, shortly after, the double bass, on which he later became a virtuoso. He was exposed to a wide variety of music in these formative years and his interests ranged from negro spirituals and gospel music, through the big band music of Duke Ellington to sophisticated chamber works and the music of the great classical composers.

Mingus made his first moves into the music business while still at school: he was invited to play with the Buddy Collette band and shortly afterwards made his debut with Lee Young. In 1941 he joined the Louis Armstrong band and this proved to be the start of an extremely successful time for him, though it was somewhat marred by Armstrong's firing him just two years later for some anti-segregationist remarks that he made while on tour in the southern states. Mingus was deeply committed to political issues, particularly racism, and, as an aggressive and highly motivated young man, he had no qualms about making his views known.

From a career point of view, the Armstrong incident did not affect his development or progression in any way. He was quickly invited to play alongside Kid Ory and

Alvino Ray and then in 1946 he joined forces with Lionel Hampton, with whom he spent two years as part of Hampton's big band; during this time he made his first recording in 1947 playing out-and-out bebop music. It was also during this period that he composed one of his most famous tunes, 'Mingus Fingers', which was frequently performed and later recorded by the Hampton Big Band. In the early Fifties he played with many of the biggest names of the jazz world, including Red Norvo, Billy Taylor, Charlie Parker, Stan Getz, Duke Ellington, Bud Powell, Fats Navarro and Art Tatum. However, in an episode reminiscent of the Armstrong incident some years previously, Mingus decided to leave the Red Norvo Trio when he discovered that he'd been replaced for a television broadcast by a white player – he was naturally widely supported on this issue. Debut Records was a new record label that he started with his friend and colleague Max Roach and it proved to be a useful channel for a number of recording projects that met with mixed reactions from the critics; the basic philosophy of the label was to manage and promote new black artists. Two years later he founded the Charles Mingus label.

In 1953 he performed in a celebrated concert at the Massey Hall, Toronto, appearing on stage with Dizzy Gillespie and Charlie Parker – this concert was such a success that the players joined forces to set up a new foundation, The Jazz Composer's Workshop. Mingus subsequently formed a new quintet centred on the ethics of this foundation, whose ambitions were to broaden the whole spectrum of jazz and to encourage the unification of the widest range of styles from all cultures and musical backgrounds.

Always an innovator, in 1960 he created the now world-famous Newport Jazz Festival which has been staged every year since its inception. However, by the mid-Sixties Mingus had run into financial and health problems and eventually became paralysed by the incurable disease amyotrophic lateral sclerosis. As a tribute to his life and work, Jimmy Carter honoured him with an award for his services to music and when he died his ashes were scattered, at his own wish, in the River Ganges. His catalogue of recordings is extensive, and more than twenty discs under his own name are currently available on CD. His autobiography *Beneath the Underdog* makes fascinating reading both for his clearly stated political views and for numerous jazz anecdotes.

RECOMMENDED LISTENING

Abstractions (The Charles Mingus Jazz Workshop)
Affinity: AFF 750 (CD)

Blues and Roots
Atlantic: 781336-2 (CD)

Immortal Concerts
Entertainers: ENTCD 236 (CD)

Reincarnation Of A Lovebird
Candid: CS 9026 (CD/LP)

Revisited
Verve: 826 496-2 (CD)

Thelonious Monk (1917–82)
(piano)

Thelonious Sphere Monk was born in Rocky Mount, North Carolina and at the age of five moved to New York with the family. He started taking piano lessons at the age of six and, being an exceptionally intelligent child, showed a particular aptitude to both the sciences and music. Ever an enquiring child, Thelonious Monk engaged in many different academic and performing arts activities. He was just twenty when he was invited to join the house band of Kenny Clarke at the celebrated Minton's Playhouse; a few years later he worked in the Coleman Hawkins band and then joined the Dizzy Gillespie Big Band.

Monk was an innovator and had a style all of his own that proved to be the inspiration for many who followed him. He started directing his own bands in the late Forties and in 1947 he undertook some recording sessions for Blue Note that are still widely acclaimed – *Genius of Modern Music* is the appropriately titled CD. Monk wrote some of his best-known tunes at this time, including ''Round Midnight', 'Ruby My Dear' and 'Well You Needn't', all of which have since become standards. Along with Dizzy Gillespie, Charlie Parker, Kenny Clarke and Bud Powell, Thelonious Monk was one of the founders of the bebop movement and it is as a composer that he is primarily remembered, although his ability on the piano was outstanding. His compositions are, in the main, formally structured but what makes them sound unusual and original is the subtle use of harmony, supporting carefully phrased melodic lines that are gripping in their intensity

– listen to 'Blue Monk', 'Off Minor' or 'Epistrophy' for three excellent examples of some of his finest works.

Monk's colleagues held him in the very highest regard. In fact, he was unanimously supported and revered by his fellow musicians even before the critics had begun to realize the importance of the man's gift to jazz. Art Blakey is quoted as saying that it was Monk who really started the bebop movement, that he came before Parker and Gillespie and was 'the first major composer in jazz since Duke Ellington'.

Also well known for his contribution to films, including *Jazz on a Summer's Day* and *Les Liaisons Dangereuses*, Monk holds the title for writing one of the most performed and recorded jazz standards of all time in the tune ''Round Midnight'. Noteworthy events of his life include a possession of drugs charge in 1951 (and a subsequent ban on performing in New York for six years thereafter) and constant ill health in his later years, which caused him to stop live performances altogether. He died of a stroke in 1982 at Englewood in New Jersey; ironically the event instigated a surge in the popularity of his music when many of the top names in jazz recorded tribute albums – Steve Lacy, Anthony Braxton and Paul Motian among many others.

RECOMMENDED LISTENING

Genius of Modern Music: Volumes 1 and 2
Blue Note: 781510 and 781511 (CD)

Monk's Music
Original Jazz Classics: OJC 084 (CD/LP/cassette)

(Monk) Plays Duke Ellington
Original Jazz Classics: OJC 024 (CD/LP/cassette)

Thelonious Monk With John Coltrane
Original Jazz Classics: OJC 039 (CD/LP/cassette)

The Unique Thelonious Monk
Original Jazz Classics: OJC 064 (CD/LP/cassette)

Jelly Roll Morton (1890–1941)
(piano, vocals)

The self-proclaimed 'Originator of Jazz', Ferdinand 'Jelly Roll' Morton was born in New Orleans on 20 October 1890 and even if one doesn't totally subscribe to his grandiose claim, it is undeniable that he played a significant role in the development of the medium of jazz. At the age of sixteen he was already playing professionally – admittedly not for very much money, as his main venues included brothels and rough pubs, but it is well documented that such experiences gave him an excellent grounding for what was to become an extraordinarily colourful life. He was an impresario who loved to take control of every aspect of a performance, down to hiring Creole musicians from New Orleans to play alongside him, and paying people to attend rehearsals in order that the final performances would be just as he wanted them to be. He was born of Creole ancestry on his father's side and this undoubtedly had a bearing on his feelings towards the disciplines of performance. He had sparse but encouraging musical tuition as a boy, mainly from a professor of music at St Joseph's Seminary College, but when his mother died (when Jelly was just fourteen years old) and he was sent away to live with an uncle, he felt the time was right to break away and start making a living.

His first jobs were actually in brothels, where good money was to be made, but we know that later on he was actively involved in music as a pianist and vaudeville act while also managing to dabble as a pimp, a music publisher, a hotelier/club owner and a boxing promoter, as well as running a tailor's shop! In 1923 he moved to Chicago where he wrote and recorded numerous ragtime piano works, the most famous of which include 'The King Porter Stomp', 'The Kansas City Stomp', 'The Pearls' and more bluesy numbers like 'Sidewalk Blues' and 'Dead Man Blues'. By the end of the Twenties he had made his way to New York where his popularity was somewhat less than in Chicago and he found himself playing mainly as a rehearsal pianist and in the pit bands for cabaret and club acts.

The famous claim to be the originator of jazz came about after he heard a radio announcer introducing W. C. Handy, the bandleader from Alabama, as 'the originator of jazz and the blues'. W. C. Handy was indeed at the forefront of the movement but, like Morton, could never be considered solely worthy of such an accolade. Jelly Roll Morton, however, a flamboyant, outrageous character who never missed an opportunity for any kind of self-promotion, was so incensed by this introduction that he immediately wrote to *Downbeat* magazine claiming the title 'originator of jazz' for himself on the grounds that he had invented jazz in 1902!

Morton put together the band known as The Red Hot Peppers, with whom he made some famous recordings in 1926, at the request of Frank Melrose. The results were stunning and in 1939 he was invited again by RCA to record as a solo artist. However, his health failed him and after a couple of heart attacks he died in a Los Angeles hospital in 1941. One of the great characters from the world of jazz, Jelly Roll Morton has left us with a fine legacy of recordings on piano rolls and his music lives on in the hands of a devoted following – among them such artists as the British trumpeter Kenny Ball and the American pianist-composer Dick Hyman.

RECOMMENDED LISTENING

The Complete Jelly Roll Morton 1926–1930
RCA Bluebird: ND 82361 (5CDs)

Gerry Mulligan (born 1927)
(baritone sax, piano, soprano sax)

Hailing from New York but raised in Philadelphia, the composer–baritone saxophonist Gerry Mulligan has carved a unique place in the jazz world as probably the finest baritone sax player of all time. He has not achieved such unanimous praise for his compositions but nevertheless has produced much fine work which reveals an astute and stylized perception of modern jazz.

Initially, Mulligan made a career as a composer, having previously taught himself to play the piano and later the saxophone; he sold his arrangements to radio stations and various small-time bandleaders. He showed such a phenomenal talent on the saxophone that he was many people's first choice on the baritone chair in a number of bands and, following a meeting with the great Gil Evans, Mulligan was invited in 1948 to play and arrange for the Miles Davis Band, where his innovative contribution to the 'cool' movement had a wide effect on all saxophonists. He went on to form a succession of his own smaller groups with such artists as Chet Baker, Zoot Sims and Jon Eardley. These were all relatively successful and other work included playing alongside Dave Brubeck, and in the Stan Getz tribute to Zoot Sims at the Chicago Festival in 1985.

Gerry Mulligan has a passionate interest in steam locomotives, even naming his tracks and albums after them: 'The Flying Scotsman' and *The Age of Steam* are well worth exploring. Still active as a player, writer and arranger, Gerry Mulligan is a virtuoso baritone saxophonist with a remarkable gift for easy swing-style soloing – one of the greatest.

RECOMMENDED LISTENING

At Storyville
Pacific Jazz: CDP 794472 (CD)

The Best of the Gerry Mulligan Quartet with Chet Baker
Pacific Jazz: CDP 795481 (CD)

California Concerts Volumes 1 and 2
Pacific Jazz: CDP 746860/746864 (CD)

Compact Jazz: Gerry Mulligan
Mercury: 830697 (CD)

Compact Jazz: Gerry Mulligan Concert Jazz Band
Verve: 838933 (CD)

Charlie Parker (1920–55)
(alto sax)

Charlie Parker was born in Kansas City and is most commonly known by his nickname 'Bird' – a shortened version of 'Yardbird' because of his passion for eating fried chicken. Kansas City was a breeding ground for jazz musicians (saxophonists in particular) with artists like Parker, Ben Webster and Lester Young all born within a four-mile radius.

Parker started to play the baritone saxophone while at the Crispus Attucks High School and for his eleventh birthday his mother gave him an alto – the instrument which so profoundly influenced the whole jazz world and with which his name became synonymous. After a couple of years he decided to drop out of school and devote his life to jazz. He practised incessantly and developed a technique and facility of breathtaking agility that itself formed an integral part of the flavour of bebop music in the Forties.

Parker's earliest experiences in the music business were rather mixed, to say the least. He soon developed a reputation as something of a wild character, drinking and taking drugs at a very early stage in his life, but musically he was very aware and learned a lot very quickly; he was soon noticed by his colleagues – some of whom resented his quick rise to fame. After gaining experience with bands fronted by George Lee, Lawrence Keyes, Harlan Leonard and Jay McShann, Parker felt confident enough to move to New York in 1939, finding work wherever he could. He was frequently invited to play at the Uptown House and this was a period when he made some very good contacts and was heard by a number of influential people in the jazz world. A couple of years later he spent more time in New York recording with McShann for Decca and in May 1941 he met Dizzy Gillespie. Over the course of the next three or four years Parker and Gillespie worked alongside each other developing the new sound of jazz known as bebop.

Besides his extraordinary facility on the saxophone, Parker had an innovative approach to improvisation, creating his solos from the top notes of the accompanying chord sequences, so that instead of focusing on the simplest versions of the chords in each tune, he would pick the ninth, eleventh and thirteenth degrees of the scales to form the basis of his solo lines. This led to a greater degree of ambiguity in his style which, to some people's ears, sounded foreign and somewhat disorientating, while to true jazz aficionados it provides the very lifeblood of his playing.

Parker's problems with heroin addiction came to a head in the mid-Forties, culminating in the summer of 1946 when he set fire to his hotel room in Los Angeles and was sent to the psychiatric wing of the LA County Jail and later to a rehabilitation centre. This period proved to have a positive effect on him and when he re-emerged on the jazz scene he was playing on top form. He made a number of excellent recordings during this time and formed a group with the trumpeter Miles Davis. He toured abroad and was well received wherever he played. However, this productive period in his life was not to continue for long. Within a matter of a year or so, Parker was suffering from cirrhosis of the liver and was extremely overweight, he was back on narcotics and in a very unstable condition. This did not appear to affect his powers of creativity and his playing in 1955 was reported to be as inventive as ever. His final performance in public was on 4 March 1955 at Birdland, the jazz club named after him, where he played on stage with the pianist Bud Powell and bassist Charles Mingus. Powell and Parker had a row on stage which resulted in Powell and Mingus storming off stage, leaving the sad figure of Parker alone in the spotlight. Charlie Parker died just eight days later.

A significant recorded legacy, clearly demonstrating Parker's true genius is now available on all formats. In addition to his undisputed influence on the course of jazz saxophone playing, he left his mark on the history of jazz by helping to create a new language in bebop. All of the recordings featuring him as a soloist are well worth exploring; a particularly interesting one is 'With Strings', which was one of his own personal favourites and one of a pair of recordings that he and Dizzy Gillespie produced in a more commercial vein.

Best of Bird on Savoy
Savoy: 650 109 (CD)

Charlie Parker
Verve: 833288 (CD)

Charlie Parker and Dizzy Gillespie
M&R: JRCD 101 (CD)

Charlie Parker At Storyville
Blue Note: BT 85103 (CD/LP)

Savoy Master Takes
RCA: ZD 70737 (CD)

Oscar Peterson (born 1925)
(piano)

The Canadian virtuoso jazz pianist, Oscar Emanuel Peterson, was born in Montreal and has since become a household name in jazz. During his years at school, Peterson studied classical piano and reportedly practised for twelve to fourteen hours each day – which may well explain why he has such a phenomenally dextrous technique. However, it was not until his mid-Twenties that Peterson really broke into the big time, having played in and around the jazz clubs throughout Canada, mainly in Montreal and Toronto. In 1949 he was 'spotted' by the talent scout and impresario, Norman Granz, who gave Peterson the opportunity to make his solo debut in the

United States. From this time on he developed a highly successful career as a soloist, as a leader of his own Trio and as a member of the Jazz at the Philharmonic concert tours, also organized by Norman Granz.

Peterson's style was firmly rooted in the swing era and he is undoubtedly a master of swing piano, bringing his own special mixture and virtuoso talent to his performances. He admits to being influenced by the other great jazz piano virtuoso, Art Tatum; another of his great heroes was Nat King Cole, to whom he attributes much of his early inspiration. Peterson's hallmarks are his ability to decorate the melodic line with impeccable dexterity and a gift for moving seamlessly through a number of different keys while retaining a definite 'bluesy' harmonic style.

Equally at home as a soloist or as an accompanist, Peterson has played with many of the giants of the world of jazz, including Louis Armstrong, Ella Fitzgerald, Lester Young, Dizzy Gillespie and Sarah Vaughan. He is familiar to audiences all around the world through his live appearances and numerous TV and radio broadcasts.

RECOMMENDED LISTENING

Compact Jazz: Oscar Peterson and Friends
Pablo: 835315 (CD)

Compact Jazz: Oscar Peterson Plays Jazz Standards
Verve: 833283 (CD)

The George Gershwin Songbook
Verve: 823249 (LP only)

Jam Session 1955
Moon: 029 (CD/LP)

Jazz at the Philharmonic, Hartford, 1953
Pablo Live: 2308240 (CD)

Django Reinhardt (1910–53)
(guitar)

Jean-Baptiste Reinhardt, later to become known as Django, is now recognized as one of the most remarkable jazz guitarists of all time. He was born in 1910 of very humble origins in a caravan in a shanty town and spent his childhood travelling with his gypsy father, a multi-talented entertainer who worked as an act in a travelling show. Django was always fascinated by music and was soon given a violin and later a guitar. However, at the age of eighteen, Django was trapped in a serious caravan fire which caused him to lose the use of two fingers on his left hand. What would have been a catastrophic blow to many simply made Django develop a unique technique for playing the guitar and a style that has since been the inspiration for many jazz guitarists who followed him.

With his brother Joseph, Django first became interested in jazz on the Côte d'Azur and the two young men frequented cafés and bars that presented live music, seizing whatever opportunities they could to perform themselves. When he moved back to Paris, Django was often to be heard playing solo in the cafés around the Montmartre area and it was during one such performance that he was noticed by a painter from Toulon, Emile

Savitry who was so taken by Django's talent that he introduced him to another French jazz star called Jean Sablon. Django continued to play on his own and as a member of several bands, including that of Sablon, until 1934 when he formed the now legendary group with Stephane Grappelli, the Quintette du Hot Club de France.

Within a very short time the group became internationally famous and they quickly produced an extensive catalogue of records, many of which are still available. The line-up of the group was unusual and had a certain novelty value as many had never heard such a combination of instruments: solo violin, solo guitar, two rhythm guitarists and double bass. After a while Django felt that it was time to move on again and, following his gypsy instincts, took off in his caravan in search of pastures new, both musically and domestically. After a brief flirtation with a big band, Django formed another quintet, this time with a French clarinettist Hubert Rostaing, until his passion for writing music took over and he decided to apply himself seriously to straight composition. The results were mixed; many of the pieces were never finished, but still surviving are a symphony and a film score for *Le village de la Colère* (1946). He also arranged a swing version of the Violin Concerto in D minor by J. S. Bach which received mixed reactions from the critics but unanimous approval from his followers.

Duke Ellington eventually tracked Django down and invited him to play with his band, which he duly did and took up the electric guitar to help him fit in with the swing, big band style that was so popular at the time. Django fitted in very well musically but although it was good to see the great man's talents demonstrated publicly again, it is generally felt that his heart was not really in what he was doing at this time. He also became involved in the bebop scene and again he met with wide acclaim but it is widely agreed that his best works were those based on folk music, such as the melancholic masterpiece entitled 'Nuages', written in 1940.

Django died in Fontainebleau in France on 16 May 1953 after a stroke. In his last years he had been invited to take part in the Norman Granz Jazz at the Philharmonic tours and had also just recorded with Pierre Michelot and Martial Solal.

RECOMMENDED LISTENING

Djangology 1949
RCA Bluebird: ND 90448 (CD/LP)

Django Reinhardt
Forlane: UCD 19001 (CD)

Swing From Paris
ASV: AJA 5070 (CD)

Swing Guitar
Jass: JCD 628 (CD)

Swing In Paris 1936–1940
Affinity: AFS 1003 (CD)

Buddy Rich (1917–87)
(drums)

Renowned as one of the finest drummers ever to have graced the world's stages, Bernard 'Buddy' Rich achieved fame as an all-round entertainer. He was born in Brooklyn, New York to parents who were heavily involved in the Broadway show scene. He was on stage from the age of four and soon developed his own act as a drummer and tap dancer. He shot to fame overnight and was obviously an extremely precocious and extraordinarily talented child, forming his own band at the age of eleven and shortly afterwards being invited to play with many top jazz artists in clubs in and around New York.

From his late teens Rich played in bands led by Harry James, Artie Shaw, Joe Marsala, and Tommy Dorsey among others and, after he had completed his military service, he rejoined the Dorsey band for a short time before striking out on his own with his own big band. He was a frequent guest at the Jazz at the Philharmonic concert tours organized by impresario Norman Granz and throughout the Fifties, in addition to staging his own big band concerts, he played and recorded with all the great names in mainstream jazz, including Oscar Peterson, Art Tatum, Lionel Hampton, Louis Armstrong, Miles Davis and Dizzy Gillespie.

A musician possessing an extraordinary gift of rhythm, Buddy Rich developed a big reputation both on and off the stage. He was an immensely powerful player who could dominate the band both through his playing, or simply with a 'look'; he surrounded himself in his later years by a band made up predominantly of young musicians and they certainly knew who was boss! Rich toured extensively throughout his life – even after having major open heart surgery. Buddy Rich was indeed larger than life – an exceptional musician and showman who remains in the history books as one of the most remarkable characters of the last few decades.

RECOMMENDED LISTENING

Class of '78
BBC Century: CJCD 832 (CD)

Compact Jazz: Buddy Rich
Verve: 833295 (CD)

Illusion
Sequel: NXT CD 181 (3CD)

Time Being
RCA:ND 86459 (CD)

Tuff Dude
LRC: CDC 7972 (CD)

Sonny Rollins (born 1930)
(tenor, soprano and alto sax)

Theodore Walter Rollins, known as 'Sonny', was born in New York City in September 1930. He took up studying the alto saxophone at the age of thirteen while at high school and although he was first inspired by hearing the jazz/rock-and-roll saxophonist Louis Jordan, Charlie Parker was probably his greatest influence.

Rollins soon became extremely proficient on the saxophone and had an easy, natural gift for improvising. He switched over to the tenor sax while still a teenager and began doing live gigs with bands in and around New York from the age of seventeen. Dexter Gordon also had a significant influence on the young Rollins, but Sonny quickly developed a style of his own which attracted the attention of some top bandleaders and jazz musicians who invited him to play alongside them; they included Thelonious Monk, Miles Davis, Tadd Dameron and Art Blakey – all before Sonny Rollins had reached the age of twenty.

During the early Fifties he was in great demand. His style was very contemporary in the true bop mode and his profound command and understanding of the essential elements of music in rhythm and harmony made him one of the most innovative improvisers around. He recorded with Miles Davis and then spent a couple of years with the Max Roach-Clifford Brown quintet, producing some highly influential recordings and giving numerous concerts and live performances. Having worked with the likes of Miles Davis, Thelonious Monk and Bud Powell, Sonny Rollins was enormously experienced in the bop style but always hankered after developing his style still further. His work with Max Roach provided the ideal platform and the results are well recorded for all to explore. Perhaps the most famous recording from this time is the blistering duo with his colleague John Coltrane in 'Tenor Madness'. Right at the end of the Fifties Rollins decided to quit live playing and spent the next two or three years studying. He has an enquiring mind and a deep interest in self-improvement and the pursuit of all things intellectual, particularly where music and his performing ability are concerned. This first period of retreat made a big impact on his playing and one can really sense the feeling of intense commitment to his music making that resulted from this profound inner searching.

On coming out of retreat in 1962, Sonny Rollins formed his own group, Sonny Rollins and Co. The personnel changed slightly over the following two or three years but featured such musicians as Jim Hall and Don Cherry on guitar and the superb drummer Billy Higgins. The year 1968 saw another retreat from public performance and Rollins spent the next three years studying in India and Japan. He came back to the jazz world and had a brief flirtation with the medium of jazz rock, which many considered an ill thought-out move. Rollins did too, it seems, and quickly went on to yet another stage in his career, which seemed to bring together all the elements of his early influences and his recent soul searching to make him a player of unique ability and extraordinary versatility. He was a member of the 1978 Milestone All Stars concert tour but a few years later decided to abandon the traditional jazz nightclub venues, preferring to make more elaborate concert performances in larger halls.

Now in his sixties, Rollins performs as a grand master of the jazz saxophone, at times demonstrating his ability to be at the cutting edge of improvisation and advanced techniques on his instrument, and at other times showing graceful lyricism or giving displays of music from his true roots harking back to the earthy style of *Don't Stop the Carnival.*

RECOMMENDED LISTENING

G Man
Milestone: 9150 (CD/LP/cassette)

A Night at the Village Vanguard Volumes 1 and 2
Blue Note: CDP 7465172/7465182 (CD)

The Quartets
Bluebird: ND 85643 (CD)

Saxophone Colossus
OJC: 291 (CD/LP/cassette)

Tour de Force
OJC: 095 (CD/LP/cassette)

Ronnie Scott, OBE (born 1927)
(tenor sax)

A name that is synonymous with jazz, Ronnie Scott has achieved fame on two counts – firstly as a fine tenor saxophonist and secondly as the owner of a couple of jazz clubs that are world-renowned. He started playing the saxophone as a schoolboy, inspired by the music of the big bands that were emerging in the early Forties. By the time he was sixteen he was a very competent player and started gigging. By 1946, still a teenager, he had already toured with trumpeter Johnny Claes when he was invited to join the celebrated Ted Heath Band, where he firmly made his mark.

He was keen to explore the world and enjoyed the touring life, playing on transatlantic cruise ships before returning to London to join the Jack Parnell Band. Scott is a strong character and natural leader; he formed his own nine-piece band and opened his own nightclub in Frith Street, Soho in the very heart of London's West End. The club has played host to many of the world's greatest performers and has also provided a welcome platform for Scott himself as the leader of a number of smaller groups.

Still to be heard occasionally at the club and at Festivals throughout the UK and sometimes in Europe, Ronnie Scott is a living legend in the jazz world. His dry, sardonic and witty monologues with which he introduces visiting acts at his club, remain fondly in the minds of his audiences. A great debt of thanks is due to this ebullient character for his vision and entrepreneurial skills in keeping a broad spectrum of jazz music in front of the public at large.

RECOMMENDED LISTENING

Never Pat A Burning Dog
RSJH: JC 012 (CD/LP/cassette)

Zoot Sims (1925-85)
(tenor sax, soprano sax)

Another of the 'light'-sounding tenor sax players who steered a course away from the harder-sounding tenor players like Coleman Hawkins, Zoot Sims was born in Inglewood, California on 29 October 1925. His early interest in music was focused entirely on the swing bands of the Thirties and indeed his first forays into the profession were as a member of the reed section for a number of small group bands playing swing band material during the Second World War. However, soon after the war was over he was invited to join the Benny Goodman band, but stayed only for a year before joining the Woody Herman Band as a member of the celebrated Four Brothers. He maintained the contact with Benny Goodman and enjoyed widespread success on a number of European tours over a period of thirty years or so, while also guesting with Stan Kenton's Band, the Jazz at the Philharmonic and Jazz at Carnegie Hall groups, and enjoying dates with Gerry Mulligan's sextet and big bands, among others.

Very much a distinguished solo player in the Lester Young mould, Zoot Sims received offers to work on numerous recording projects throughout his career. He also had the honour, in 1961, of being the first US performer to play a season at Ronnie Scott's club in London.

Famous initially for his tenor sax playing, he also took up the soprano saxophone in the early 1970s and developed a style of performance that maintained all the traits of economy and understatement which he had brought to his tenor playing and which were quite different from the blistering displays of virtuosity from other soprano players around him. Sims was a truly great musician whose career came to a sad end in 1985 when he died of cancer shortly after his final tour of Scandinavia.

RECOMMENDED LISTENING

Live at Ronnie Scott's 1961
Fresh Sound: FSR-CD 134 (CD)

Warm Tenor
Pablo: 2310-831 (CD)

Zoot!
Original Jazz Classics: OJC 228 (CD/LP/cassette)

Zoot Sims and the Gershwin Brothers
Original Jazz Classics: OJC 444 (CD/LP/cassette)

Zoot Sims in Paris
EMI/Pathé Jazztime: 794125 (CD)

Art Tatum (1909–56)
(piano)

Art Tatum was an enormously talented and highly respected all-round musician whose virtuoso technique on the piano few have equalled, before or since. He was born in Toledo, Ohio in 1909 and was virtually blind from birth. One effect of this disability was that when he began learning the piano in his early childhood, his extraordinary powers of concentration revealed a precocious talent that stunned the world. He could play by ear at the age of three and later learned to read music in braille. He started performing in public at the age of thirteen and made his solo recording debut at the age of twenty-three in New York – this first recording caused quite a stir, as his rendition of 'Tiger Rag' was thought by many to have been played by two people, such was the phenomenal display of virtuosity.

Tatum's earliest influences included the legendary Fats Waller and the other exponents of the 'stride piano' technique, of which Art Tatum later became the un-rivalled master. He was able to play at such blistering speed that the style took on a completely new dimension and paved the way for a new genre. Tatum's unusual subtleties in harmonic development and his ability to play extraordinary rhythms independently with each hand, secured him many followers from the bebop school; among them the saxophonists Charlie Parker and John Coltrane were very much impressed and influenced by Tatum's new vision of harmony and rhythm. Indeed, many of the world's finest musicians have acknowledged the genius of Art Tatum: Count Basie described him as the eighth wonder of the world!

From the early Thirties, Tatum built a highly success-ful career as a soloist in clubs in Hollywood, Chicago and New York and later, in 1943, he formed his own trio with the drummer Tiny Grimes and double bassist, Slam Stewart. This trio developed an excellent reputation and Tatum led a happy life until his untimely death of uraemia at the age of forty-seven. During the last five years of his life, Tatum was very busy performing solo and with his trio in clubs and concert halls throughout the United States. Norman Granz organized a number of recording sessions during which Tatum recorded some one hundred and twenty tracks for solo piano, in addition to other material with people like Ben Webster, Lionel Hampton, Benny Carter, Buddy Rich and Jo Jones. He gave his last concert in 1955 and died in Los Angeles the following year.

RECOMMENDED LISTENING

Classic Early Solos 1934–1939
MCA: GRD 607 (CD)

The Complete Capitol Recordings, Volumes 1 and 2
Capitol: 7928662/7928672 (CD)

The Complete Pablo Group Masterpieces
Pablo: 401 (6 CDs)

The Complete Pablo Solo Masterpieces
Pablo: 4404 (7 CDs)

The Standard Transcriptions
Music and Arts: CD 673 (CD)

Sarah Vaughan (1924–90)
(vocals)

Sarah Lois Vaughan stands as one of the great icons of jazz singing, alongside Ella Fitzgerald, Betty Carter and Billie Holiday. She was born in Newark, New Jersey on 27 March 1924 and begin singing and playing the piano at the age of six. Her big break came when she won an amateur talent contest at the Apollo Theatre in Harlem, after which she was asked to join Earl Hines's band as the second pianist and lead vocalist. Billy Eckstine was at this time a member of the Earl Hines band but when he left he managed to persuade Sarah to join him. She was soon in great demand as a solo singer and cabaret artist in the New York clubs. She always had an ear for what was commercial and had a string of hits throughout the Forties and Fifties which brought her artistry to a very wide audience. On a more serious musical note, she also had a deep interest in bebop and delighted in working with artists like Dizzy Gillespie and Charlie Parker – one great example of such work is the track 'Lover Man' which she recorded with Dizzy Gillespie in 1946.

A singer of great virtuosity, it is not surprising that her ability to improvise was one of her great strengths. She developed her own brand of 'scat' singing and 'Sassy', as she affectionately became known, was remarkably influential in this area. One of the reasons for this unique ability is her perseverance in developing improvisations in a true bebop style, rather than simply decorating a melody line as many jazz singers do. Betty Carter once commented that Sarah Vaughan could have made a very fine operatic singer and this may well have been the case – her quality of tone, exceptional vocal range and musical instincts place her at the very top of many people's list of great singers of the twentieth century.

RECOMMENDED LISTENING

Compact/Walkman Jazz: Sarah Vaughan
Mercury: 830699 (CD/cassette)

Compact/Walkman Jazz: Sarah Vaughan with Clifford Brown
EmArcy: 814641 (CD)

The Divine Sarah Vaughan: The Columbia Years 1949–1953
Columbia: 465597 (CD/cassette)

Sarah Vaughan Live!
Mercury: 832572 (CD)

Send in the Clowns
Pablo: 2312-230 (CD/LP/cassette)

Ben Webster (1909–73)
(tenor sax)

One of my own personal favourite jazz artists, Benjamin Francis Webster was born in Kansas City, Missouri on 27 March 1909 and has left his mark on the world of jazz primarily for his breathy, sensual artistry on the tenor saxophone. He was a natural musician who, from a very early age, displayed his enormous potential on a variety of instruments, notably the violin and piano, before taking up the saxophone; this was at the suggestion of Budd Johnson, a talented reed player who worked with Louis Armstrong, Earl Hines and later with people like Dizzy Gillespie.

Webster took to the saxophone immediately and soon after joined the Young Family Band (featuring Lester Young and his father who both helped Ben on his way with tips on how to play). By the early Thirties, Ben Webster had made quite an impact and had a glittering career ahead of him. Everyone was taken by the sheer expressiveness of his sound and his talents were used to great effect in stunning solo contributions to tracks like 'Lafayette' and 'Moten Swing' with the Bennie Moten band in 1931.

In 1940 Duke Ellington invited Webster to join his band and it was during this period that Ben Webster's true style, as we primarily remember it today, was developed. He brought a breath of fresh air to the reed section of the Ellington Band; some of his finest moments can be heard in classics like 'Cottontail' and 'Until Tonight', with 'All Too Soon' being among many people's favourites from this wonderful period in the band's history. Webster fell out with Ellington one night when, having been allowed to play the piano in a couple of numbers, he stayed in the chair too long. This greatly displeased his bandleader and in the row that followed Webster cut up one of Ellington's suits! Thankfully the feud didn't last for ever: some four or five years later Webster rejoined the Ellington band after playing for a variety of lesser-known band leaders and forming his own band with whom he did a lot of live gigs in the smaller clubs in and around New York.

He moved to the West Coast so that he could stay in close contact with his mother but following her death he moved back to New York, frequenting all the major clubs on the jazz scene. By 1964, however, he was very conscious of the new trends and decided to spend more time in Europe so as to be a part of the action. He moved to Copenhagen, which served as a good base for his activities. He made numerous friends and fans in Scandinavia, one of whom, Billy Moore Jnr, set up the Ben Webster Foundation after the maestro's death, in an effort to support the jazz music cause in Sweden.

From the early Fifties Ben Webster's career progressed and he assumed many of the characteristics and personality traits that people automatically associate with jazz musicians – heavy drinking, unreliability (he was known for being up to three days late for a gig!), womanizing and frequenting whore-houses. Nevertheless his playing went from strength to strength and with his own small groups he made a number of excellent recordings – all well worth listening to, although there is a strong school of aficionados who claim that his finest work was done in the Duke Ellington Band. Explore the recordings and make your own mind up – whatever anyone may say, Ben Webster has undeniably left us with a truly identifiable sound.

The Blanton–Webster Years
  (with the Duke Ellington Band)
RCA: Bluebird 85659 (3 CDs/4 cassettes)

Live in Amsterdam
Charly: 168 (CD)

Soulville
Verve: 833551 (CD)

Stormy Weather
Black Lion: BLCD 760108 (CD)

There Is No Greater Love
Black Lion: BLCD 760151 (CD)

Lester Young (1909–59)
(tenor sax)

Born into a musical family, Lester Young spent much of his early life in New Orleans and became one of the all-time great tenor saxophonists. Lester Young ('Prez', as he was affectionately named by his close friend Billie Holiday) is famous for creating a style of saxophone playing that remained inimitably his when all around him were forging new styles. Considered old-fashioned by the critics, Young was able to produce a round sound with just a hint of edge when required. His individuality did not always serve to his advantage, but he was a gentleman of the saxophone loved by all for his great charm. He first really made a name for himself in the Count Basie Band of the mid-Thirties, having served his apprenticeship in bands led by Art Bronson, Walter Page (The Blue Devils) and Bennie Moten. He stayed in the Basie band for about five years; one of his reasons for leaving was a desire to go his own way and ultimately to lead a band of his own.

Freelancing was not as easy as he had hoped and Prez returned to the Basie band for a short stint in 1943. He was then conscripted to the army, a period in his life which had severe repercussions, leaving him tormented and mentally scarred until his untimely death in 1959. However, he found his own way of dealing with the problems – often resorting to drinking and heavy smoking, and later to drugs – and had a relatively successful decade or so working on the Jazz at the Philharmonic concert series organized by Norman Granz. His style was decidedly different from his colleagues, who included his old sparring partner and rival saxophonist, Coleman Hawkins.

Periods of depression and ill health dogged his life from the mid-Forties onwards and although Lester Young was always widely respected, he felt that he never achieved the recognition or rewards that he deserved. His disappointment caused further heavy drinking and drugtaking and he spent much time in the company of his close friend and soul mate, Billie Holiday. Things went from bad to worse in the late Fifties and, just when there was an exciting new album planned with Gil Evans, Prez had a heart attack in a hotel room in Paris and died at the age of fifty. Thankfully, a marvellous recorded legacy is left for us to enjoy – his many live concert recordings give a marvellous insight into the artistry of one of the greatest saxophonists ever.

Lester Young in Washington, D.C. 1956:
  Volumes 1 and 2
Pablo Live: CD 2308219/CD 2308225 (CD)

Live at the Royal Roost 1948
Jazz Anthology: 550092 (CD)

The President: Volumes 1 and 2
Jazz View 029/030 (CD)

Prez's Hat: Volumes 1–4
Philology: 214 W6-9 (LP)

Joe Zawinul (born 1932)
(keyboards)

Josef Zawinul is perhaps best known (with saxophonist Wayne Shorter) as co-founder of the group Weather Report. Born in Vienna in 1932, Zawinul was brought up in a family who had a strong interest in music, particularly of the folk and gypsy variety. He was given an accordion to play at the age of six (an instrument which he plays to this day) and progressed to the piano towards the end of the Second World War when the family was evacuated from Vienna to Czechoslovakia. It was apparent even at this early stage that he had a remarkable talent and at seventeen he won a scholarship to study at the Berklee School of Music in Boston. He didn't stay in school for long – the extrovert trumpeter Maynard Ferguson invited him to join his band, and Joe Zawinul went straight out on the road for eight months.

During the late Sixties several significant events helped to place Zawinul among the leading jazz musicians of the time: he worked a lot with Julian 'Cannonball' Adderley (for whom he wrote the tune 'Mercy, Mercy, Mercy') and was involved as a writer and performer with Miles Davis for such all-time classic albums as *In A Silent Way, Bitches Brew, Live Evil* and *Big Fun*. In fact, the title track 'In A Silent Way' came from Zawinul's pen.

It was with the band Weather Report that Zawinul really achieved mass popularity. The band presented a very broad spectrum of music encompassing many styles, ranging from free modal jazz to electro-funk and taking in some extraordinary ethnic and folky influences along the way – it all added up to an eclectic mix that many (including myself) found highly enjoyable.

Still active, and regarded as something of a legend as both a composer and a keyboard player, Zawinul has made many fine recordings, all of them strongly recommended. An extraordinarily versatile and inventive musician, he can be heard on an interesting album with saxophonist Ben Webster entitled *Soulmates*; my own particular favourites focus largely on his earlier works and those he made with Weather Report.

Recommended Listening

The Beginning
Fresh Sound: FSR CD 142 (CD)

Black Market
CBS: 81325 (LP)

Heavy Weather
CBS: 81775 (CD)

I Sing the Body Electric
Columbia: 468207 (CD)

Weather Report
Columbia: 468212 (CD)

CHAPTER FIVE

Where To Go To Hear Jazz

Many people still think of jazz as a minority interest with no real mass appeal, yet it is astonishing to see how many regular jazz venues and festivals there are all around the world. These are to be found not only in the main cities but in some of the most unlikely and far-flung places.

The festival scene is perhaps the most exciting – every year hundreds take place throughout Europe and the United States. They vary in size from events like the Brecon Jazz weekend in mid-Wales (which presents an amazing line-up of traditional and mainstream jazz performers each year) to the world renowned North Sea Festival in The Hague and the Montreux and Nice Jazz Festivals, which each attract over eight hundred musicians to perform to audiences many, many times that number. Some festivals take place in idyllic settings – none more so than Perugia (some 140km north of Rome, in Italy) where the beauty of the location, as well as the exceptionally high quality of the performers, has won the festival a truly international reputation. Perugia is an exquisite medieval town, nestling in the hills above the Tiber valley – the views are magnificent and the music takes place in the market square, in churches and in a curious small theatre. So whether you fancy jazz in an Italian market square or blues on a boat on the River Clyde in Glasgow, your tastes and requirements are catered for.

As with all art forms, music in particular, there really is nothing like experiencing the 'live event' and the atmosphere at most jazz concerts is compelling. It is also at the smaller festivals that the jazz giants of tomorrow are given their first opportunities to present their music to enthusiastic and discerning audiences and at these events you will often find the best-known names side by side with up-and-coming new talents.

Here follows a brief directory featuring a cross-section of the most respected larger clubs and festivals, together with a selection of the smaller but no less stimulating events that happen throughout the world. It is impossible for such a list to be completely comprehensive but it will at least give you some ideas. If there is any difficulty in tracking down these or other jazz events, I've always found local information centres and tourist offices to be of great help. With the festivals, I've given the time of year in which these usually take place, but the exact dates vary from year to year, so do check before you go – wherever possible a contact number is given. The festivals are listed in chronological order.

UK Festivals

Mid/late April
Jersey Jazz Festival
(Tel: 0534 43425)

Late April/early May
Giant Hertfordshire Jazz Festival
(Tel: 0707 281537/8)

Early May
Cardiff Bay Jazz Festival
(Tel: 0222 340501)

Solihull Arts Festival
(Tel: 021 704 6962)

Mid-May
Coventry Jazz Festival
(Tel: 021 454 7020)

Keswick Jazz Festival
(Tel: 0684 566956)

Portsmouth Festival
(Tel: 0705 834182)

Portsmouth Arts Festival 'Blues Weekend'
(Tel: 0705 834182)

Late May/early June
Beaumaris Festival (Anglesey, North Wales)
(Tel: 0248 810930)

Glossop Jazz Festival
(Tel: 0457 865412)

Guinness Jazz and Blues Festival at Hollywood (Belfast)
(Tel: 0232 427888)

Newcastle upon Tyne Jazz Festival
(Tel: 091 232 7079)

Late June
Appleby Jazz Festival
(Tel: 07683 51052)

China House Jazz Festival, Plymouth
(Tel: 0626 832060)

Glastonbury Jazz Festival
(Tel: 0839 668899)

Oliver Cromwell International Jazz Festival
  (Upton-upon-Severn)
(Tel: 0684 593254)

Real Ale Jazz and Blues Festival (Lichfield)
(Tel: 0543 257557)

Early July
Aberystwyth Jazz Festival
(Tel: 0970 623232)

Bracknell Festival
(Tel: 0344 484123)

Glasgow International Jazz Festival
(Tel: 041 227 5511)

South Bank Jazz and Blues Festival, Grimsby
(Tel: 0472 242000)

Swanage Jazz and Blues Festival
(Tel: 0929 422885)

Mid-July
Wigan International Jazz Festival
(Tel: 0942 825677)

WOMAD Festival, Rivermead (Reading)
(Tel: 0225 744044)

Late July/early August
Buxton Festival of Jazz Music
(Tel: 0298 72190)

Mid-August
Brecon Jazz Festival
(Tel: 0874 625557)

Late August
Brighton Jazz Festival
(Tel: 0273 712379)

Clacton Jazz Festival
(Tel: 0255 423400)

Kilvert's Jazz Festival, Hay-on-Wye
(Tel: 0487 821042)

Wirral International Jazz Festival
(Tel: 051 639 3559)

Late August/early September
Bude Jazz Festival
(Tel: 0288 356360)

Edinburgh International Jazz Festival
(Tel: 031 557 1642)

Early September
The Long Weekend (Clevedon, Somerset)
(Tel: 0275 343210)

OUTSIDE IN Festival, Crawley
(Tel: 071 439 0807)

Mid-September
Bath Jazz and Blues Festival
(Tel: 0225 463362)

Brentwood Jazz Festival
(Tel: 0277 200300)

Rotherham Jazz Festival
(Tel: 0709 558785)

Early October
Soho International Jazz Festival
(Tel: 071 734 6112)

Mid-October
Dunoon Jazz Festival
(Tel: 0369 3785)

November
Belfast Festival at Queens
(Tel: 0232 665577)

A SELECTION OF THE MAIN UK VENUES THAT PROMOTE JAZZ CONCERTS

Here follows a list of the main UK venues that promote live jazz in one form or another. The details have been compiled from a variety of publications and directories – wherever possible a telephone number for information is supplied.

England

LONDON
100 Club
100 Oxford Street, London, W1N 9FB
(Tel: 071 636 0933)

606 Club
90 Lots Road, London, SW10 0QD
(Tel: 071 352 5953)

The Bulls Head
373 Lonsdale Road, Barnes Bridge, London, SW13 9PY
(Tel: 081 876 5241)

Jazz Café
5 Parkway, Camden Town, London, NW1 7PG
(Tel: 071 916 6060)

Jazz Rumors – The Vortex Jazz Bar
7 Farleigh Road, London, N16 0GJ
(Tel: 071 249 3342)

Palookaville
13a James Street, London, WC2 8BT
(Tel: 071 240 5995)

Pizza Express
10 Dean Street, London, W1V 5RL
(Tel: 071 437 9595)

Regent's College
The Inner Circle, Regents Park, London, NW1 4NS
(Tel: 071 486 0141)

Ronnie Scott's Club
47 Frith Street, London, W1V 6HT
(Tel: 071 439 0747)

Tenor Clef
1 Hoxton Square, London, N1 6NU
(Tel: 071 729 2476)

The Tulse Hill Tavern
150 Norwood Road, London, SE24 9AY
(Tel: 081 674 9754)

SOUTHERN ENGLAND
Andover

Cricklade Theatre
Charlton Road, Andover, Hants., SP10 1EJ
(Tel: 0264 365698)

Bournemouth

The Showbar
Pier Approach, Bournemouth, BH2 5AA
(Tel: 0202 551685)

Brighton

Brighton Jazz Club
214 Kings Road Arches, Brighton, Sussex, BN1 1NB
(Tel: 0273 600175)

Burgess Hill

The Martlett's Hall
Civic Way, Burgess Hill, West Sussex, RH15 9NN
(Tel: 0444 242888)

Chiselhurst

The Bulls Head
Royal Parade, Chiselhurst, Kent, BR7 6NR
(Tel: 081 467 1727)

Gosport

Gosport Jazz Club
177 Stoke Road, Gosport, Hants., PO12 1SE
(Tel: 0705 522834)

King's Langley

The Rose and Crown
60 High Street, King's Langley, Herts., WD4 9HT
(Tel: 09277 62462)

Maidstone

Pizza Express
32 Earl Street, Maidstone, Kent, ME14 1PS
(Tel: 0622 753162)

Ramsgate

Churchills Jazz Club
19–22 The Paragon, Ramsgate, Kent, CT11 9JS
(Tel: 0843 587862)

Weybridge

The Hand and Spear
The Heath, Heath Road, Weybridge, Surrey, KT13 8TX
(Tel: 0932 845035)

SOUTH-WEST ENGLAND

Bristol

The Albert
1 West Street, Bristol, Avon, BS3 3NN
(Tel: 0272 661968)

The BeBop Club
The Bear, Hotwells Road, Bristol, Avon, BS8 4SF
(Tel: 0272 268385)

Cirencester

The Brewery Arts Centre
Brewery Court, Cirencester, Gloucestershire, GL7 1JH
(Tel: 0285 657181)

Falmouth

Falmouth Arts Centre
Falmouth Arts Centre, Church Street, Falmouth,
  Cornwall, TR11 3DT
(Tel: 0326 314566)

Plymouth

Plymouth Jazz Club
Astor Hotel, 14-22 Eliot Street, Plymouth,
    Devon, PL1 2PS
(Tel: 0752 225511)

The Ordulph Arms, Kilworthy Hill, Tavistock,
    Devon, PL19 0AW
(Tel: 0822 615048)

Sherborne

Sherborne Jazz Club
Half Moon Yard, Sherborne, Dorset, DT9 3LN
(Tel: 0935 812074)

Taunton

Taunton Jazz Club
The Eagle Tavern, South Street, Taunton,
    Devon TA1 3AF
(Tel: 0823 286049)

Tavistock see Plymouth

Totnes

Dartington Hall
Totnes, Devon, TQ9 6EJ
(Tel: 0803 865864)

MIDLANDS

Birmingham

The Bear
500 Bearwood Road, Birmingham,
  W. Midlands, B66 4BX
(Tel: 021 429 1184)

Midlands Arts Centre (Studio Theatre and The Hexagon)
Cannon Hill Park, Birmingham, W. Midlands, B12 9QH
(Tel: 021 440 3838)

Ronnie Scotts
258 Broad Street, Birmingham, W. Midlands, B1 2HE
(Tel: 021 643 4525)

Waterworks Jazz Club
Old Philipians Association Ltd, 20 Waterworks Road,
Edgbaston, Birmingham, B16 9AL
(Tel: 021 454 0212)

Burton

Burton Jazz Club
Boathouse Inn, Stapenhill, Burton,
  W. Midlands, DE15 9HF
(Tel: 0283 38831)

Coventry

University of Warwick Arts Centre
University of Warwick, Coventry,
  W. Midlands, CV4 7AL
(Tel: 0203 524524)

Derby

The Wherehouse
110a Friargate, Derby, Derbyshire, DE1 1EX
(Tel: 0332 381169)

Leicester

Phoenix Arts Centre
11 Newarke Street, Leicester, LE1 5SS
(Tel: 0533 (554854)

Lichfield

Lichfield Arts Centre
Bird Street, Lichfield, Staffs., WS13 6PR
(Tel: 0543 262223)

Northampton

The Derngate Centre
19–21 Guildhall Road, Northampton, NN1 1DP
(Tel: 0604 248111)

Nottingham

The Old Vic Tavern
22 Fletchergate, Nottingham, E. Midlands, NG1 2FZ
(Tel: 0602 585914)

EASTERN ENGLAND

Brentwood

Monkeys Jazz Club
The Hermit Centre, Shenfield Road, Brentwood,
  Essex, CM15 8AG
(Tel: 0277 218897)

Chelmsford

Chelmsford Jazz Club at the Cramphorn Theatre
Cramphorn Theatre, Fairfield Road, Chelmsford,
    Essex, CM1 1JG
(Tel: 0245 495028)

Colchester

Colchester Arts Centre Jazz Club
Colchester Arts Centre, Church Street, Colchester,
    Essex, CO1 1NF
(Tel: 0206 577301)

King's Langley

Rose and Crown
60 High Street, King's Langley, Herts., WD4 9HT
(Tel: 09277 62462)

Luton

The 33 Arts Centre
33–35 Guildford Street, Luton, Beds., LU1 2NQ
(Tel: 0582 419584)

Potters Bar

Wyllyotts Centre
Wyllyotts Place, Darkes Lane, Potters Bar,
    Herts., EN6 2HN
(Tel: 0707 45005)

St Albans

Red Note
Maltings Arts Centre, St Albans, Herts., AL1 3HL
(Tel: 0727 844222)

Southend-on-Sea

The Blue Note Jazz Club
Cliffs Pavilion, Station Road, Southend-on-Sea,
  Essex, SS0 7RA
(Tel: 0245 436330)

Welwyn Garden City

Herts Jazz at the Fairway Suite
Fairway Suite, Panshanger Golf Complex,
  Welwyn Garden City, Herts., AL7 2ED
(Tel: 0707 339507)

NORTH-WEST ENGLAND
Burnley

The Mechanics Arts and Entertainment Centre
Manchester Road, Burnley, B11 1JA
(Tel: 0282 30055)

Chester

Alexander's Jazz Theatre
2 Rufus Court, Off Northgate Street, Chester, CH1 2JW
(Tel: 0244 340005)

Liverpool

Bluecoat Arts Centre
Bluecoat Chambers, School Lane, Liverpool,
  Merseyside, L1 3BX
(Tel: 051 708 8877)

Kirklands Wine Bar
13 Hardman Road, Liverpool, L1 9AS
(Tel: 051 707 0132)

Manchester

Band on the Wall
25 Swan Street, Manchester, M4 5JQ
(Tel: 061 834 1786)

Eastside Jazz Café
85 Oldham Street, Manchester, Lancs, M4 1LW
(Tel: 061 834 4266)

Preston

The Lamb
83 Church Street, Preston, Lancs., PR1 3BS
(Tel: 0772 254478)

Southport

Southport Arts Centre
Lord Street, Southport, Lancs., PR8 1DB
(Tel: 0704 540011)

NORTH-EAST ENGLAND
Bradford

Alhambra Studio
St George's Hall, Bingley Arts Centre, Bradford,
   West Yorks., BD7 1AJ
(Tel: 0274 752375)

The Wool Exchange
Bank Street, Bradford, W. Yorks., BD1 1LE
(Tel: 0274 752000)

Darlington

Darlington Arts Centre
Vane Terrace, Darlington, Co. Durham, DL3 7AX
(Tel: 0352 483168)

Hartlepool

The Grand Hotel
Swainson Street, Hartlepool, Cleveland, TS24 8AA
(Tel: 0642 562104)

Hull

The Spring Street Theatre
Spring Street, Hull, Humberside, HU2 8RW
(Tel: 0482 23638)

Newcastle upon Tyne

Corner House Hotel
Heaton Road, Heaton, Newcastle upon Tyne,
   Tyne and Wear, NE6 5RP
(Tel: 091 265 9602)

The Live Theatre
27 Broad Chare, Newcastle upon Tyne,
   Tyne and Wear, NE1 3DQ
(Tel: 091 261 2694)

Scarborough

The Mermaid
Foreshore Road, Scarborough, Yorks., YO11 2UZ
(Tel: 0723 379818)

Sheffield

The Charnwood Hotel
Sharrow Lane, Sheffield, S. Yorks., S11 8AA
(Tel: 0742 738678)

The Leadmill
Leadmill Road, Sheffield, S. Yorks., S9 1PJ
(Tel: 0742 754500)

York

York Arts Centre
St Johns, Micklegate, York, N. Yorks., YO1 1JG
(Tel: 0904 627129)

Scotland

Aberdeen

The Lemon Tree
5 West North Street, Aberdeen, AB2 3AT
(Tel: 0224 642230)

Dumfries

Mabie House Hotel
Troqueer Road, Mabie, Dumfries, DG2 8HB
(Tel: 0387 63188)

Glasgow

13th Note
80 Glassford Street, Glasgow, G1 1UR
(Tel: 041 887 4733)

The Village Theatre
Maxwell Drive, East Kilbride, G74 4HQ
(Tel: 0355 248669)

Paisley

Paisley Arts Centre
New Street, Paisley, PA1 1EZ
(Tel: 041 887 1010)

Wales

Cardiff

The Four Bars Inn (the Welsh Jazz Society)
Castle Street, Cardiff, CF1 2BS
(Tel: 0222 340591)

Llantwit Major

The Tythe Barn Theatre
St Donats Arts Centre, St Donats Castle, Llantwit Major,
    S. Glamorgan, CF6 9WF
(Tel: 0446 794848)

Prestatyn

Nant Hall Hotel
Prestatyn, Clwyd, LL19 8RT
(Tel: 0745 853901)

Rossett

Alyn Hotel
Station Road, Rossett, Clwyd, LL12 LHE
(Tel: 0244 570368)

St Asaph

The Farmers Arms
The Waen, nr St Asaph, Clwyd, LL17 0DY
(Tel: 0745 582190)

Swansea

Ellington's – The Duke of York
Princess Way, Swansea, S. Glamorgan, SA1 5LW
(Tel: 0792 772776)

Northern Ireland

The Front Page
Donegall Street, Belfast, BT1 2DX
(Tel: 0232 324924)

The Rotterdam Bar
54 Pilot Street, Belfast, BT1
(Tel: 0232 746021)

Ardhowen Theatre
Enniskillen Arts Centre, Dublin Road, Enniskillen,
    Fermanagh, BT74 6BR
(Tel: 0365 325440)

A SELECTION OF INTERNATIONAL VENUES AND FESTIVALS

The New York Club Scene

55 Bar
55 Christopher Street, east of 7th Avenue South
(Tel: 929 9883)

The Blue Note
131 West 3rd Street east of 6th Avenue
(Tel: 475 8592)

Carlos I
432 6th Avenue at 9th Street
(Tel: 982 3260)

Condon's
117 East 15th Street
(Tel: 254 0960)

Fat Tuesdays
190 3rd Avenue at 17th Street
(Tel: 533 7902)

The Knitting Factory
47 East Houston
(Tel: 219 3055)

Sweet Basil
88 7th Avenue South
(Tel: 242 1785)

The Village Corner
142 Bleecker Street
(Tel: 473 9762)

The Village Gate
160 Bleecker Street
(Tel: 475 5120)

The Village Vanguard
178 7th Avenue South at 10th Street
(Tel: 255 4037)

Visiones
125 MacDougal Street
(Tel: 673 5576)

Festivals Abroad

USA
The New Orleans Jazz and Heritage Festival
(April/May)
Tel: (504) 522 4786

DENMARK
Aarhus International Jazz Festival (July)
Tel: 45 86 13 43 44

Copenhagen Jazz Festival (July)
Tel: 45 33 93 20 13

EIRE
Guinness Jazz Festival – Cork (October)
Tel: 010 353 21 270463

Monaghan Festival (September)
Tel: 010 353 47 81122

FRANCE
Festival Django Reinhardt (June)
Tel: 64 24 64 82

Festival de Jazz Antibes/Juan les Pins (July)
Tel: 9333 9564

Festival de Jazz de Paris (October/November)
Tel: 1 4783 3358/4056 0709

Festival Jazz au Vienne (July)
Tel: 7453 6030

La Grande Parade du Jazz (July)
Tel: 1 46 21 08 37

FINLAND
Pori International Jazz Festival (July)
Tel: 358 39 411 565

GERMANY
Jazz Fest Berlin (November)
Tel: 30 254 890

ITALY
Jazz Land (July)
Tel: 6 759 7851

Jazz a Trento (March/May)
Tel: 461 986 448/236 462

Ravenna Jazz Festival (June/July)
Tel: 544 405 666

Reggio Emilia Jazz (March/May)
Tel: 522 434 244

Umbria Jazz (July)
Tel: 75 62432

NETHERLANDS
Drum International Jazz Festival (July)
Tel: 020 204 313

Jazz Marathon Gronigen (December)
Tel: 050 672 120

Jazz Mecca (October/November)
Tel: 070 350 20 34

North Sea Jazz Festival (July)
Tel: 31 70 350 2034

NORWAY
Molde International Jazz Festival (July)
Tel: 47 72 16 000

POLAND
International Jazz Festival (Summer)
Tel: 22 277 904/276 731

PORTUGAL
Jazz de Lisboa (November)
Tel: 1 804 243

SPAIN
Encuentros Europeos en el Camino de Santiago
  (November)
Tel: 81 581 928

Festival Internacional de Jazz, Granada (November)
Tel: 58 274 000

Festival Internacional de Jazz, Mallorca (November)
Tel: 71 719 671/715 745

SWITZERLAND
International Jazz Festival, Berne (April/May)
Tel: 031 972 5005

International Jazz Festival, Zurich (Autumn)
Tel: 1 216 3169/3111/3294

Montreux Jazz Festival (July)
Tel: 021 963 4663

CHAPTER SIX

Building A Jazz Record Collection

Having read thus far, you've probably already identified some stylistic preferences of your own and, with the aid of the Recommended Listening lists and the *Get Into Jazz* album, may even have started to explore the enormous catalogue of jazz that is currently available on CD, record and cassette. Here follows a brief review of ten of my own favourite jazz albums that I hope you too may enjoy.

Almost all the recommendations are available on compact disc and many are also available on record and cassette. Many of the major record companies are now concentrating their efforts on re-mastering old recordings for the digital format of compact disc and some are even already making versions for digital compact cassette (DCC), but I have not included any references to DCC titles here as there are simply not sufficient DCC system owners to warrant inclusion at this stage.

The jazz catalogue is vast and when one considers that

artists like Louis Armstrong, Duke Ellington and Miles Davis are each represented by over a hundred compact disc recordings, one can appreciate that a life-long study of their recorded works is not beyond the realms of possibility! Many of the jazz recordings available are of live concerts in venues ranging from Carnegie Hall and the Montreux Jazz Festival to smaller clubs and venues in Italy and Scandinavia, and including jazz landmarks like Ronnie Scott's Jazz Club in Frith Street, London; although the quality of these live recordings does vary, I have made a serious effort to include the best all-round performances combined with recordings of good technical quality.

So here follows my short list; it's a totally subjective collection that features both undisputed jazz classics and one or two more controversial choices – controversial in that they are commercial products designed to pander to mass market tastes rather than to the connoisseur. I don't see anything wrong with such a scenario, so long as people enjoy what they hear and I hope that, as a result of exploring some of the recommendations in this book, you will be able to explore the vast catalogue of recorded jazz works for yourself and build your own library of favourites.

1 LOUIS ARMSTRONG: *Hot Fives and Sevens Volumes 1–3*
JSP 312CD, JSP 313CD, JSP 314CD

These recordings are as famous within the music industry as they are throughout the jazz record-buying public.

When one considers that they were made some sixty years ago, their ability to stand the test of time is remarkable. Armstrong plays superbly throughout the whole set of three discs, even if at times the sound gets a little rough and out of tune in places – but who can be worried by such things when the whole spirit of these recordings, made by his 'studio only' bands (The Hot Fives and Hot Sevens), convey as wonderfully exuberant an approach to music making as you can find in any genre.

Among my favourite tracks in the series (and there are many) are 'Wild Man Blues', 'Jazz Lips' and the hauntingly beautiful 'Knockin' A Jug', although it seems almost invidious to single out any. Find a copy for yourself and make your own mind up – you won't be disappointed.

These albums cannot be recommended too strongly and are available on CD and on LP in a variety of transfers and re-mastered versions. To my ears the JSP CDs (as quoted in the catalogue numbers above) sound the best and are widely available.

2 JOHN COLTRANE: *The Major Works of John Coltrane*

Impulse!: GRD 21132 (2CDs)

Coltrane is among my favourite jazz musicians and while there are countless albums spanning his whole career, this one has a very special place in my collection. The tracks come from sessions dating from 1965, and some confusion surrounds the release of much of the material found here. It seems that some of the tapes had been muddled up and that Coltrane had given the go-ahead for one version of

'Ascension' to be released but that the record company made a mistake and put out an unapproved version. Such things occasionally happen and the two versions have here been brought together for all to enjoy.

By and large the performances show Coltrane in fine form, although the recording quality varies between tracks on occasions. Much of the music may be described as 'difficult' or inaccessible – this is not light, easy-to-listen-to jazz by any stretch of the imagination – but it is worth bearing in mind that the tracks were recorded at a time when Coltrane was perhaps at the peak of his ability to improvise coherently and thus they provide an insight into the extraordinary talent of the man.

Listen, too, for the delightful interjections of Joe Brazil on flute in the track 'Om' – inspired by Eastern religious chanting and Coltrane's deep affinity to matters spiritual. The track 'Selflessness' is also worthy of special mention, showing the band in exceptional form – these are two albums well worth exploring if Coltrane's magic and the hard-sounding music of the mid-Sixties appeals to you.

3 MILES DAVIS: *Kind of Blue*
CBS: 32109

At the top of the list of many a jazz buff's favourite albums, *Kind of Blue* is among the very best of Miles Davis's recorded output. It came almost exactly one year after another outstanding album, *Milestones*, which surely must also be regarded as an extremely significant disc and worthy of a place in the collection.

In *Kind of Blue* Miles adopted the style which became

known as 'modal jazz' i.e. the utilization of modal scale patterns to form the basis of his improvisations, which here show the great man at his finest. Other artists performing alongside Miles Davis are the pianist Bill Evans (who plays with such beauty of tone colour and subtle voicing of harmonies it must have proved a source of extraordinary inspiration to the featured soloists) and tenor saxophonist John Coltrane.

This is one not to be missed on any account!

4 MILES DAVIS: *Mellow Miles*
Columbia: 469440 (2CDs)

Although the purists may disagree with me here, I cannot ignore an album that has given countless people an enormous amount of pleasure. The collection features Miles Davis performing a string of great tunes, ranging from some quite early works to more recent offerings and taking in classic tracks like ''Round About Midnight', 'So What' (which is also featured on *Kind of Blue* – *see* above), 'Summertime' and 'Human Nature'.

This kind of album is a boon for those who do not want to delve deep into the vast Miles Davis catalogue but who just want to enjoy hearing the master playing many of his more soulful hits from previous albums in a very attractive package. It's been a big hit for the record company concerned and I understand there may be more of the same to come. This is late-night listening par excellence.

5 STAN GETZ: *The Girl From Ipanema*
Verve: 823611 (4CDs)

Personally, I'm very fond of jazz with Latin influences and the collection presented here by Stan Getz, also featuring Joao Gilberto and his wife Astrud, Antonio Carlos Jobim, Gary Burton, Tommy Williams, Steve Kuhn and others, gives a comprehensive insight into the music of this genre.

At all times led from the front by Stan Getz, whose sound and whole style of playing is so well suited to this music, many of the tracks also feature the husband and wife team of the Gilbertos singing in the distinctive timbre which has become almost synonymous with songs like the title track and 'Desafinado', which is on the CD and cassette *Get Into Jazz*.

This is a superb collection of discs, attractively packaged by Verve, in which I constantly hear new elements to the playing and the music appears ever fresh – a set that will provide hours of enjoyment over the years both to serious jazz lovers and to those who enjoy 'easy'-sounding background jazz.

6 ELLA FITZGERALD: *The George and Ira Gershwin Songbook*
Verve: 821024-2 (3CDs)

Although this collection is to the best of my knowledge currently available only as an import in the UK (but these things can change) this set of three CDs features Ella Fitzgerald in absolutely magnificent form, singing alongside The Nelson Riddle Orchestra.

The quality of the recordings is uniformly excellent, especially considering they were made some thirty-three years ago and it almost goes without saying that the performances are also quite superb. Ella Fitzgerald is a natural interpreter of this kind of repertoire and her obvious affinity to these songs shows, from the most popular tunes that we all know and love through to some less well-known, but equally enchanting tracks. Among the latter is a track entitled 'You've Got What Gets Me', which has now become one of my own personal favourites.

Nelson Riddle's orchestra makes a beautiful contribution to the whole. The arrangements never fail to please the ear and to keep one's interest, without detracting from the songs themselves, while the instrumental playing throughout is impeccable.

There are over three hours of music to enjoy here and this set of three CDs would be a jewel to have in any jazz record collection.

7 KEITH JARRETT: *Expectations*

Columbia: 467902

Not perhaps an album that would spring to everyone's mind as being at the top of a Keith Jarrett list of favourites, but one from which I have derived much enjoyment. Released on the Columbia label, it has only recently been released on CD and sees Jarrett unusually playing as part of a large group; the other musicians notably include Sam Brown and Charlie Haden on guitar and bass respectively, with Paul Motian on drums and Dewey Redman on tenor saxophone. Some wonderful Latin percussion sounds emanate from the dextrous hands of the incomparable Airto Moreira and a string and brass section complete the team for this recording.

What I particularly like about the disc is the fusion of styles presented: one is quite used to hearing Keith Jarrett records that very much follow a particular course or thought process within the music-making, but here we see him in free mood, obviously enjoying the opportunity to get involved in straight jazz, jazz rock, Latin, gospel and lush-sounding arrangements, all of which show him in exceptional form.

Many people may be unaware of Jarrett's abilities on other instruments – on a couple of tracks he is to be heard playing soprano saxophone, a little bit of organ and percussion. This is a fascinating recording from one of the all-time greats who is still producing much very fine work.

8 PAUL MOTIAN: *On Broadway, Volumes 1 and 2*

JMT: 834430 and 834440

Paul Motian plays here in a line-up not dissimilar to that of the Keith Jarrett recording above, with Bill Frisell and Charlie Haden on guitar and bass, and Joe Lovano on tenor saxophone. These two albums (both available individually) were made in the last five years and, for me, represent some of the finest 'accessible' jazz material produced in the last ten years.

Many of the tunes will be familiar – 'Body and Soul' and Gershwin's 'Someone To Watch Over Me', for example – however, it is the treatment and the sheer inventiveness of the arrangements by these four musicians that have me captivated from beginning to end.

Paul Motian is a wonderful drummer and leader of the group and one gets the feeling that these guys really enjoyed their time together making these two very fine CDs.

9 JOHN McLAUGHLIN: *Extrapolation*

Polydor: 841598

The Penguin Guide to Jazz cites this record as 'one of the finest jazz records ever made in Europe' and, indeed, I would hesitate to disagree, for this album shows off the talents of the guitarist John McLaughlin in the very best light. The recording was made in the early part of 1969 and features just three other musicians: John Surman (soprano and baritone saxophone), with Brian Odges and Tony Oxley on bass and drums respectively. The music here is extremely innovative – at times it is peaceful and beautifully meditative, while at others the furious technical virtuosity of the guitarist leaves one speechless with amazement.

McLaughlin's recorded output is extensive and there is a fascinating catalogue to explore in addition to the tracks found on this album. Not to be missed are *The Inner Mounting Flame* and, perhaps less obviously popular, the album he made with Kai Eckhardt, Dominique De Piazza and Trilok Gurtu, entitled *Qué Alegría* which is to be found on the Verve label.

10 CHARLIE PARKER: *The Charlie Parker Story*
Savoy: SV 0105

Recorded on 26 November 1945 this album, featuring many of Charlie Parker's greatest hits, can be said to represent the very zenith of his playing career. The CD contains many out-takes and incomplete performances and one can really get a sense of how these recordings were actually made. For those who do not wish to listen every time to the false starts and breakdowns, the ID numbers on the CD can be programmed to play just the complete versions of the tunes, which include 'Now's The Time', 'Billie's Bounce', 'Ko-Ko', 'Meandering' and 'Warming Up a Riff'.

Playing with Parker on these sessions are the two kings of the trumpet Miles Davis and Dizzy Gillespie, while Bud Powell, Curley Russell and Max Roach provide the admirable rhythm section. It is generally accepted that the contributions made by Miles Davis do not feature his finest playing and there may be a number of reasons for this – the one that springs immediately to my mind is the rather obvious lack of empathy with and understanding of what Parker was trying to achieve musically. This is perhaps borne out by the different direction which Davis took shortly after these sessions.

Nevertheless, this recording presents an exceptional collection of talented musicians playing, by and large, outstanding material; this particular recording allows us to eavesdrop on the session – a real gem for the collection.

Bibliography

Louis Armstrong: *Satchmo – My Life in New Orleans* (Da Capo, New York, 1986)

Gerald Arnaud and Jacques Chesnel: *Masters of Jazz: Chambers Compact Reference* (Chambers, 1991)

Joachim Berendt: *The Jazz Book* (Paladin, 1984)

Ian Carr, Digby Fairweather and Brian Priestly: *Jazz – The Essential Companion* (Paladin, 1988)

Samuel Charters and Leonard Kundstadt: *Jazz – A History of the New York Scene* (Da Capo, New York, 1981)

Richard Cook and Brian Morton: *The Penguin Guide to Jazz* (Penguin, 1992)

John Humphries (ed.): *The Official Music Master Jazz Catalogue* (John Humphries, 1990)

Colin Larkin (ed.): *The Guinness Who's Who of Jazz* (Guinness Publishing, 1992)

Humphrey Lyttelton: *The Best of Jazz* (Robson Books, 1978 onwards)

Humphrey Lyttelton: *I Play As I Please* (MacGibbon & Kee, 1954)

Humphrey Lyttelton: *Second Chorus* (MacGibbon & Kee, 1958)

Charles Mingus: *Beneath the Underdog* (Weidenfeld & Nicholson, 1971)

Ross Russell: *Bird Lives* (Quartet, 1973)

Herb Sanford: *Tommy & Jimmy – The Dorsey Years* (Ian Allan, 1972)

Frank Tirro: *Jazz – A History* (Dent, 1979)

Author's Note

The catalogue numbers that appear in the Recommended Listening lists have been drawn from personal collections and consultation with *The Penguin Guide to Jazz on CD, LP and Cassette*. The availability of all the recordings cannot be guaranteed as record companies are constantly withdrawing, reissuing and recompiling their material. Every effort has been made to ensure the accuracy of the information herein.

INDEX

Index

Track titles are shown in quotes. Unless otherwise stated, titles shown in italics are albums. For people with many references, **bold** page numbers show the main ones.

GET INTO OPERA
by Chris Cracker

*Pavarotti in the Park, The Three Tenors in Rome . . .
the magnificent world of opera has never been more
popular.*

GET INTO OPERA is a comprehensive,
easy-to-follow guide to the wonderful music available
to us either at home or in the great opera houses
around the world.

GET INTO OPERA introduces you to:

★ Your Starter Top Ten
★ Story outlines for several of the great operas
★ Where to next? Recommended operas to enjoy
★ The celebrated Composers, Stars and Directors
★ A whirlwind tour of the grand opera houses around
  the world

A follow-up to the bestselling GET INTO
CLASSICAL MUSIC, this essential guide brings to
life the music and drama of some of the greatest works,
and will enable everyone to truly appreciate and enjoy
the magnificent world of Opera.

A Bantam Paperback
0 553 40539 X

GET INTO CLASSICAL MUSIC
by Chris Craker

GET INTO CLASSICAL MUSIC is an easy-to-read guide to classical music, aimed at everyone who has been moved by the magic of Vivaldi's Four Seasons or Puccini's *Nessun Dorma*.

GET INTO CLASSICAL MUSIC will bring the fascinating world of classical music to life – unveiling the myths and mystique surrounding an art form that has, until now, been appreciated by so few.

GET INTO CLASSICAL MUSIC offers you:

★ Your Starter Top Ten
★ The Top 50 Composers
★ The Top 10 Performers
★ Recommended listening – what to try and when to try it
★ A guide to famous Film and Television music
★ A brief look at the world of Opera
★ A guide to the Instruments of the Orchestra

GET INTO CLASSICAL MUSIC will help you put a name to all the wonderful music you hear but can't easily identify – a truly accessible guide to the best of the classics.

A Bantam Paperback
0 553 40440 7

GET INTO
JAZZ

We have compiled a special collection of the major pieces of music featured in this book. *Get Into Jazz,* available on CD and cassette, consists of the original recordings as described in Chapter 2, Your Starter Selection.

To obtain the CD or cassette by post, simply complete this order form and send a cheque or postal order, made payable to *Music Men Products*, to the address given below. Please allow 28 days for delivery. (Overseas customers are asked to send the sterling equivalent and to add £1.50).

Get Into Jazz Cassette @ £5.99 each   £.........
Get Into Jazz Compact Disc @ £9.99 each   £.........

Also available by post
Get Into Classical Music Cassette @ £5.09 each   £.........
Get Into Classical Music Compact Disc @ £8.99 each £.........
Get Into Opera Cassette @ £5.99 each   £.........
Get Into Opera Compact Disc @ £9.99 each   £.........
(All prices include postage and packing)   TOTAL: £.........

Our address is:
Music Men Productions Ltd
PO Box 2807
London W6 0JW

Please print your name and address clearly on the order form and attach it to your payment:

Name: ....

Address: ....

....

.........................Postcode............